Scotland's leading educational publishers

S1 to National 4
BIOLOGY
PRACTICE QUESTION BOOK

leisure &

S1 to N4 BIOLOGY
PRACTICE QUESTION BOOK

© 2018 Leckie & Leckie Ltd

00114062018

10 9 8 7 6 5 4 3 2 1

ISBN 9780008263638

Published by
Leckie & Leckie Ltd
An imprint of HarperCollins*Publishers*
Westerhill Road, Bishopbriggs, Glasgow, G64 2QT
T: 0844 576 8126   F: 0844 576 8131
leckieandleckie@harpercollins.co.uk   www.leckieandleckie.co.uk

Special thanks to
Jouve (layout and illustration); Ink Tank (cover design);
Project One Publishing Solutions (project management);
Anna Clark (copy-edit); Jess White (proofread)

A CIP Catalogue record for this book is available from the British Library.

Acknowledgements
Cover © Attila JANDI / Shutterstock.com; P30 Goat © WilleeCole
Photography / Shutterstock.com; Tomatoes © Martyn F. Chillmaid /
Science Photo Library; Stem cells © Andrea Danti / Shutterstock.com;
DNA Profile ©T-flex / Shutterstock.com

Whilst every effort has been made to trace the copyright holders, in cases where this has been unsuccessful, or if any have inadvertently been overlooked, the Publishers would gladly receive any information enabling them to rectify any error or omission at the first opportunity.

Printed and bound by CPI Group (UK) Ltd, Croydon, CR0 4YY

Introduction   **iv**
Skills of scientific inquiry   **v**

CELL BIOLOGY

1	Cells	1
2	Cell division	4
3	DNA function and profiling	6
4	DNA, genes and chromosomes	7
5	Therapeutic use of cells	9
6	Enzymes and their use in industry	12
7	Microorganisms	15
8	Microorganisms in industry	18
9	Photosynthesis	21
10	Limiting factors in photosynthesis	24
11	Respiration	26
12	Controversial biological procedures	30

MULTICELLULAR ORGANISMS

13	Body systems	31
14	Role of technology in monitoring health	35
15	Body defences against disease and the role of vaccines	38
16	Fertilisation and embryonic development	41
17	Reproduction and survival	43
18	Propagating and growing plants	45
19	Commercial use of plants	48
20	Genetic information and inheritance	50
21	Growth and development	54
22	Maintaining stable body conditions	60

LIFE ON EARTH

23	Biodiversity, sampling and distribution of living organisms	64
24	Interdependence	68
25	Impacts on biodiversity	70
26	Nitrogen cycle	72
27	Adaptations for survival	75
28	Chemicals and food production	78
29	Fertilisers	81
30	Learned behaviour	85

ANSWERS
https://collins.co.uk/pages/scottish-curriculum-free-resources

Introduction

About this book

This book provides a resource to support you in your study of biology. This book follows the structure of the Leckie and Leckie *S1 to National 4 Biology Student Book*.

Questions have been written to cover the Key areas in the Units of National 3 Biology and National 4 Biology and the Biology Experiences and Outcomes (Es and Os) of Curriculum for Excellence (CfE) Science at 3rd and 4th levels.

Features

This exercise includes coverage of

Each chapter begins with references to the **N3** or **N4** key area and the curriculum level, **CL3** or **CL4**, and the Es and Os code it covers.

This exercise includes coverage of:
N3 Structure and variety of cells
CL3 Body systems and cells SCN 3-13a

Exercise questions

The exercises give a range of types of questions. There are questions practising the demonstration and application of knowledge, and questions practising skills of scientific inquiry.

 Identify **one** example of how a human activity changes an abiotic factor and could affect biodiversity.

 The deforestation of tropical rainforests continues to cause great concern in some parts of the world because of its impact on biodiversity.

In the 5 years between 2000 and 2005, Africa lost 3300 hectares per year. Asia lost 2800 hectares per year and South America lost 4000 hectares per year.

a Present this information in a table.

b Calculate the total number of hectares of rainforest that were lost between 2000 and 2005 inclusive. (Remember: each of the figures given is **per year**.)

Hint

Where appropriate, **hints** are provided to give extra support.

 For more information on experimental controls see page vii.

Answers

Answers to all questions are provided online at:
https://collins.co.uk/pages/scottish-curriculum-free-resources

Skills of scientific inquiry

The table below shows the various skills of scientific inquiry practised in the book.

The following pages support the answering of skills questions. To help you with the skills questions it's best to have graph paper, a ruler, calculator and a sharp pencil. Highlighter pens can also be handy.

Skill	Meaning	Page
1 Selecting	Selecting information from graphs, charts and text	v
2 Presenting	Presenting information as graph and charts	vi
3 Processing	Processing information using calculations	vi
4 Planning	Planning or designing experiments including controls, variables and reliability	vii
5 Concluding	Drawing valid conclusions from experimental results	viii
6 Predicting	Making predictions based on evidence from experimental results	viii
7 Evaluating	Identifying strengths and suggesting improvements to weaknesses in experiments	viii

This section provides hints for the questions about skills of scientific inquiry listed above.
Follow the order of the steps in the diagram: ① red, to ② green, to ③ blue, to ④ purple, to ⑤ orange.

Skill 1   Selecting information

You should be able to select relevant information from text, tables, charts, graphs and diagrams. The following example shows how to select information from a **bar chart**.

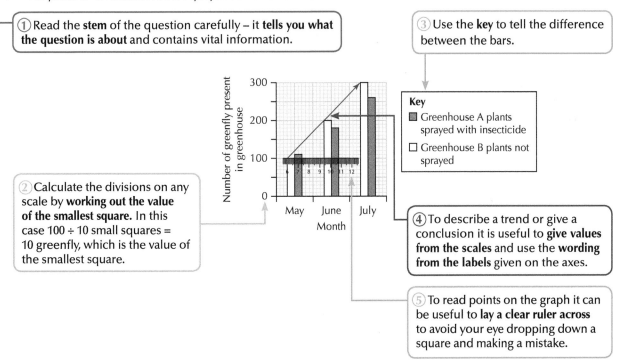

The bar chart below shows how the numbers of greenfly present in two identical greenhouses changed over 3 months. The plants in Greenhouse A were sprayed with insecticide but those in Greenhouse B were not.

① Read the **stem** of the question carefully – it **tells you what the question is about** and contains vital information.

③ Use the **key** to tell the difference between the bars.

Key
■ Greenhouse A plants sprayed with insecticide
□ Greenhouse B plants not sprayed

② Calculate the divisions on any scale by **working out the value of the smallest square.** In this case 100 ÷ 10 small squares = 10 greenfly, which is the value of the smallest square.

④ To describe a trend or give a conclusion it is useful to **give values from the scales** and use the **wording from the labels** given on the axes.

⑤ To read points on the graph it can be useful to **lay a clear ruler across** to avoid your eye dropping down a square and making a mistake.

Q *Describe how the number of greenfly present in Greenhouse B changed between May and July.*

A *The number of greenfly increased steadily from 100 in May to 300 in July.*

Q *State the number of greenfly present in Greenhouse A in June.*

A *180*

Skill 2 Presenting information

You should be able to **present** information by **completing** a line graph, bar chart or pie chart. The following example shows how to complete a **line graph**.

The effect of temperature on the rate of respiration in yeast was investigated. The results are shown in the table.

Q *On the grid, complete the line graph to show how the rate of respiration is affected by temperature.*

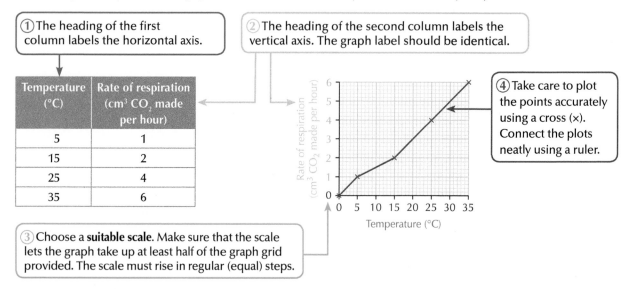

① The heading of the first column labels the horizontal axis.

② The heading of the second column labels the vertical axis. The graph label should be identical.

④ Take care to plot the points accurately using a cross (×). Connect the plots neatly using a ruler.

③ Choose a **suitable scale**. Make sure that the scale lets the graph take up at least half of the graph grid provided. The scale must rise in regular (equal) steps.

Temperature (°C)	Rate of respiration (cm³ CO₂ made per hour)
5	1
15	2
25	4
35	6

Skill 3 Processing

This example shows how to calculate **averages**, **percentages** and **ratios**.

During a survey of a habitat, the number of dandelion plants in each of five quadrats was counted. The results are shown in the table below.

Q a i *Calculate the **average** number of dandelions per quadrat.*

ii *Calculate the **percentage** of the total dandelions found which were in quadrat 3.*

Quadrat	Number of dandelions
1	6
2	8
3	⑦
4	5
5	9

A a i $6 + 8 + 7 + 5 + 9 = 35$

① Work out the total of all the data values.

$35 \div 5 = 7$

② Divide the total by the number of data values in the set.

ii $\frac{7}{35} \times 100 = 20\%$

③ Find the number in quadrat 3 (7). Divide it by the total of all the values. Multiply the answer by 100 to get the percentage.

Q b *Calculate the **ratio** of the numbers of dandelions in quadrat 1 to those in quadrat 2.*

Quadrat	Number of dandelions
1	⑥
2	⑧
3	7
4	5
5	9

A b *6, 8*

① Find the values for quadrats 1 and 2.

2

② Find the largest number which divides evenly into both values.

$6 \div 2 : 8 \div 2$

$3 : 4$

③ Divide both numbers by the largest number you found to get the ratio in its simplest form. Use a colon (:) to express the ratio.

Skill 4 Planning

You should be able to plan an experiment including the control of **variables**, ensuring **reliability**, and using a **control**.

The diagram shows a method to investigate the effect of **light intensity** (independent **variable**) on the rate of photosynthesis in pondweed (dependent **variable**).

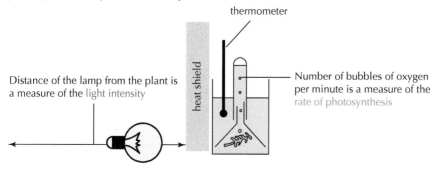

All other variables **must be kept constant** including temperature of the water.

Keeping all other variables constant ensures that any changes in the rate of photosynthesis must be caused by the change in light intensity and not by other factors.

You will often be asked to **identify variables** which must be kept the same. Common variables include temperature or pH and masses, volumes and concentrations of substances in the experiment.

Experiments such as this are **repeated** so that **reliability** is improved. Reliability is a measure of the confidence in the results.

Sometimes, experiments have a built-in **control** which helps to make conclusions valid.

> Hint   A valid conclusion is a fair conclusion which can be drawn from experimental results.

In an experiment, starch was mixed with saliva in a test tube at 20 °C and 15 minutes later there was no starch present, as shown below.

Experimental method without control

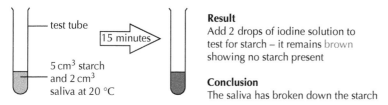

Result
Add 2 drops of iodine solution to test for starch – it remains brown showing no starch present

Conclusion
The saliva has broken down the starch

The conclusion that saliva had broken down the starch is **invalid** – the starch might simply have broken down due to the effect of the 20 °C temperature or even because of its contact with the glass of the test tube. To be sure that it was the saliva causing the breakdown, a control tube should be included, as shown below.

Experimental method with control

Experiment

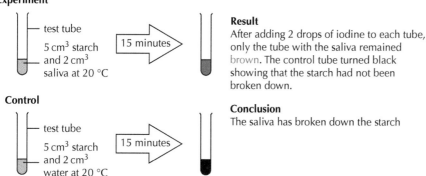

Result
After adding 2 drops of iodine to each tube, only the tube with the saliva remained brown. The control tube turned black showing that the starch had not been broken down.

Conclusion
The saliva has broken down the starch

The conclusion that saliva had broken down the starch is now **valid** – the only difference between the tubes was the presence of saliva so it must have been the saliva which produced the difference in the results.

Skill 5   Concluding

You should be able to **draw conclusions** from experimental results.

The graph shows the results of an experiment which aimed to investigate how the rate of photosynthesis was affected by increasing light intensity.

Q *Draw a **conclusion** about the effect of light intensity on the rate of photosynthesis.*

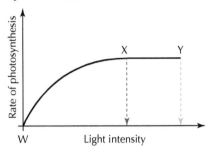

A *As the light intensity increases, the rate of photosynthesis increases between **W and X** but as the light intensity increases further, the rate of photosynthesis remains constant between **X and Y**.*

Skill 6   Predicting

You should be able to make a **prediction** from a set of experimental results. This involves thinking about what would happen if the experiment were tried in a different situation.

Q *Predict the rate of photosynthesis which would be expected if the light intensity was increased to **point Z** on the graph.*

A *2 units*

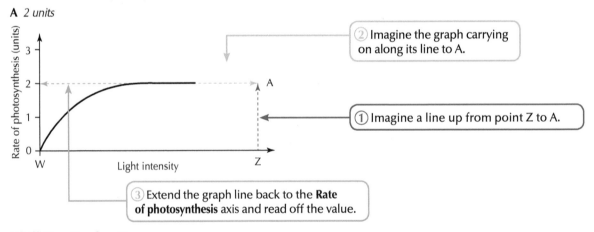

② Imagine the graph carrying on along its line to A.

① Imagine a line up from point Z to A.

③ Extend the graph line back to the **Rate of photosynthesis** axis and read off the value.

Skill 7   Evaluating

You should be able to **evaluate** an experiment to identify strengths and weaknesses and suggest improvements.

The diagram shows apparatus designed to show the effect of light intensity on the rate of photosynthesis.

Q *Evaluate this experiment by identifying a strength and suggesting a method of improving a weakness.*

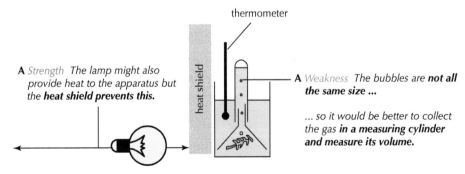

A *Strength* The lamp might also provide heat to the apparatus but the **heat shield prevents this.**

A *Weakness* The bubbles are **not all the same size ...**

... so it would be better to collect the gas **in a measuring cylinder and measure its volume.**

1 Cells

This exercise includes coverage of:

N3 Structure and variety of cells

CL3 Body systems and cells SCN 3-13a

1   Name **two** cell structures that are found in all living cells.

2   The diagram shows a cell from an animal.

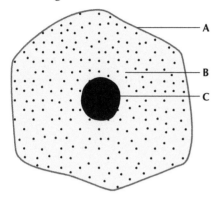

Name structures **A**, **B** and **C**.

3   The diagram shows a cell from a plant root.

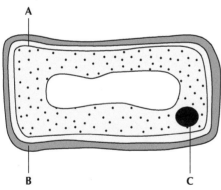

Name structures **A**, **B** and **C**.

4   The diagram shows a cell from the green part of a plant leaf.

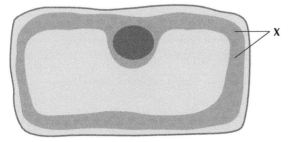

Name the structures shown at **X** which give the green cell its colour.

5 The diagram shows a cell of a microorganism.

Name the type of microorganism shown.

6 The list shows some cell structures found in human cells.

    A nucleus

    B cell membrane

    C cytoplasm

a Which letter is a structure that controls the entry and exit of substances from cells?

b Which letter is a structure that contains the genetic information of the cell?

7 The list shows some cell structures found in green plant cells.

    A large vacuole

    B cell wall

    C chloroplast

a Which letter is a structure that carries out photosynthesis?

b Which letter is a structure that gives a plant cell shape and support, and prevents it bursting when water enters?

8 Select the structures from the list which would be found in plant cells but not in animal cells.

    cytoplasm   chloroplast   cell membrane   vacuole

9 The diagrams show three different human cells.

        X   Y   Z

Identify the cells by choosing from the list.

    cheek cell   sperm cell   red blood cell

10 Humans use the cells of microorganisms to make useful substances.

a Name **one** substance that is made using yeast.

b Name the type of microorganism used to make yoghurt and cheese from milk.

11 The diagram shows cells viewed across the field of a microscope.

Calculate the average width of a cell.

Hint	For more information on how to calculate an average see page vi.

Field of view = 360 units

12 A piece of onion skin was viewed under a microscope and the lengths of 50 individual cells were measured.

The chart shows the number of cells of different lengths found.

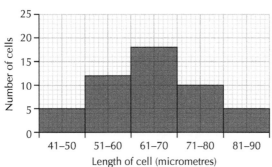

a State how many cells were 51–60 micrometres long.

b State how many cells were longer than 70 micrometres.

13 The graph shows the number of bacterial cells in a culture over a 12-hour period.

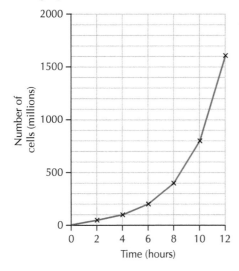

a Select the time at which there were 200 million cells in the culture.

b Select the number of cells present at the end of the 12-hour period.

c Calculate the number of cells produced every hour between 0 and 4 hours.

Hint   For more on how to select information from a line graph see page v.

2 Cell division

This exercise includes coverage of:

N4 Cell division and its role in growth and repair

CL4 Body systems and cells SCN 4-13a

1 The diagram shows a human cell during cell division.

    a Name the structure labelled **X** on the diagram.

    b Give **two** reasons why cells in a human undergo cell division.

    c Bacteria also undergo cell division.

       Give the reason why bacterial cells undergo cell division.

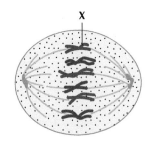

2 The diagram shows stages in cell division.

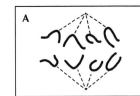

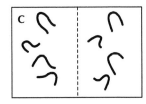
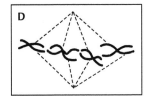

    a Give the order in which the stages **A** to **D** would occur.

    b Describe the effect that uncontrolled cell division might have on the health of a person.

3 Copy and complete the following sentences, **choosing** the word from each choice bracket to give a correct statement.

    The daughter cells produced by cell division have a chromosome number that is (**different from / identical to**) their parent cell.

    The daughter cells are genetically (**different from / identical to**) their parent cell.

4 The table shows the number of cells in a bacterial colony over a period of time.

Time (hours)	Number of living cells present (hundreds)
0	2
2	4
4	16
6	60

On a separate piece of graph paper, draw a line graph to show the number of cells against time.

> **Hint** For more information on how to draw a line graph see page vi.

5 Calculate how many bacterial cells would be present in a culture if:

a a single bacterial cell divided every 30 minutes for 3 hours

b a single bacterial cell divided every 20 minutes for 3 hours.

6 As part of an investigation into the effects of a disinfectant on the growth of a species of bacteria, a scientist set up the following dishes.

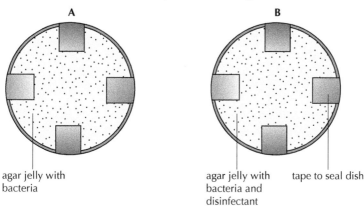

agar jelly with
bacteria

agar jelly with   tape to seal dish
bacteria and
disinfectant

The dishes were kept warm for 5 days, then checked for bacterial growth.

a Give **two** variables that should be kept the same for each dish so that valid conclusions about the disinfectant can be made.

b Explain how dish **A** acts as a control in the experiment.

> Hint For more information on experimental controls see page vii.

c Suggest why the dishes were taped as shown in the diagram.

d The scientist counted the number of bacterial colonies that had grown on each dish and the results are shown in the table.

Dish		Number of colonies after 5 days
A	Without disinfectant	60
B	With disinfectant	15

  i On a piece of graph paper, draw a bar chart to show the results of the investigation.

> Hint For more information on how to present information see page vi.

  ii Calculate the percentage reduction in bacterial colonies when disinfectant was added to the agar.

> Hint For more information on how to calculate a percentage see page vi.

  iii 1 Give **one** conclusion that can be drawn from the results given.

     2 Suggest **one** improvement to the method that could make the conclusion more reliable.

> Hint For more information on how to improve reliability in an experiment see page viii.

3 DNA function and profiling

1 The diagram shows a molecule found in human cells.

  a Name the molecule shown.

  b Give the location in a human cell where molecules such as this would be found.

  c Certain regions of these molecules are called genes.

  State what is meant by a **gene**.

2 DNA can be investigated to make DNA profiles.

Give **two** examples of the use of DNA profiles.

3 Give **one** example of a function of protein in the human body.

4 The diagram shows DNA profiles made during an investigation of a murder.

The police are investigating two suspects in the case and found two different blood samples at the crime scene.

  a Give **one** conclusion which could be drawn from the DNA profile evidence.

  b Decide if that evidence should be enough to convict anyone in this case and give a reason for your answer.

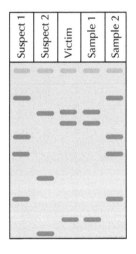

5 DNA profiles were made during an investigation into the paternity of a baby.

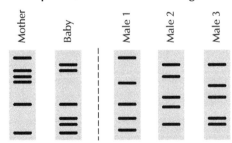

Identify the male who could be the father of the baby and explain your choice.

4 DNA, genes and chromosomes

1 Name the molecule shown here which contains genetic information.

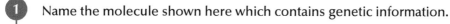

2 The diagram shows a display of the 46 human chromosomes.

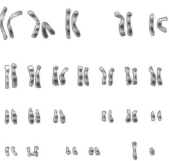

Describe what a chromosome is.

3 The diagram shows a chromosome and the position of one gene.

position of one gene

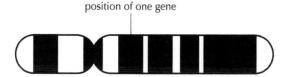

Name the substance coded for by a single gene.

4 Name the structure in a plant cell that contains chromosomes **and** identify the letter which shows this structure in the diagram.

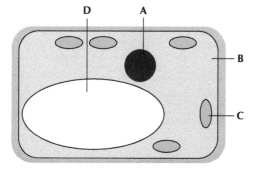

5 Place the following in order of size, with the smallest first.

      chromosome   cell   gene   nucleus

6 James and John are brothers.

Give the reason why the two brothers are unique individuals.

7 Albino mice have white coats. They don't have the protein that makes most mice grey.

 albino

 grey

Suggest what might be causing the absence of the grey protein in albino mice.

8 Haemophilia is an example of a genetic disease in which an affected person lacks a protein that clots their blood.

Explain what causes genetic diseases such as haemophilia.

9 The table shows the number of chromosomes in the cells of different species.

Species	Number of chromosomes
human	46
cat	38
dog	78
horse	64

Present this information as a bar chart on a separate piece of graph paper.

10 Read the passage and answer the questions that follow.

> The Human Genome Project (HGP) was started in 1987. Its aim was to find the positions of the human genes on the chromosomes and to read the genetic code of each gene. The reasons for doing the project were to identify the 4000 genes that were thought to be responsible for genetic diseases and to develop treatment of these through gene therapy.

a Give the date when the HGP was started.

b Give **one** aim of the HGP.

c State the number of genes that were thought to cause genetic diseases.

d Name the type of treatment now being developed following the completion of the HGP.

5 Therapeutic use of cells

1. The table describes some of the stages in the production of human insulin by bacteria.

Stage	Description
1	modified plasmid inserted into bacterium
2	bacteria grown and insulin produced
3	insulin gene used to modify bacterial plasmid
4	insulin extracted and purified
5	gene for insulin removed from human cell

a Copy and complete the flow chart by adding numbers from the table to show the correct order of these stages. The first stage has been completed for you.

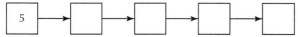

b Give the term used for the process of modifying bacteria to produce a human protein.

c Apart from insulin, name **one** other substance that is made in this way.

2. The diagram shows a bacterial cell that has been genetically modified to produce a human protein.

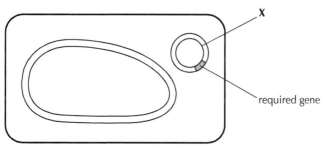

a Name structure **X** into which the required gene has been inserted by genetic engineering.

b Suggest where the required gene may have been obtained.

3 The diagram shows several possible fates of an embryonic stem cell.

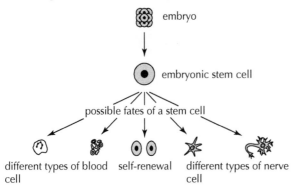

a Describe what happens during self-renewal.

b Embryonic stem cells are unspecialised.

Explain what is meant by this statement.

c Name the process by which an embryonic stem cell becomes a blood cell.

4 During a bone marrow transplant, a patient receives stem cells from the donor's bone marrow.

Describe what happens to these stem cells once they are in the patient's body.

5 Researchers in France are testing a way of making artificial skin from stem cells.

Give the properties of stem cells which allow them to produce artificial skin.

6 The histogram shows the percentage of a population with diabetes in different age groups.

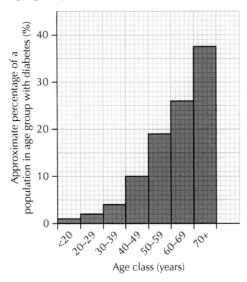

a Give the percentage of people aged 40–49 years who have diabetes.

b Describe how the percentage of the population with diabetes changes with age.

7 The graph shows the number of scientific books and articles on stem cells published in the UK between 2000 and 2008. The use of stem cells in medicine and research has continued to advance.

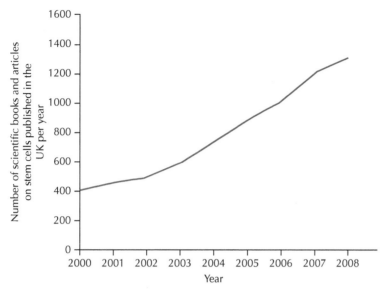

a i Describe how the number of publications on stem cells changed over the period.

ii Suggest a reason for this change.

b Predict how the number of publications would have been expected to change between 2008 and 2016.

8 The bar chart shows the results of the use of stem cell therapies on 60 stroke patients in a clinic over a period of one year.

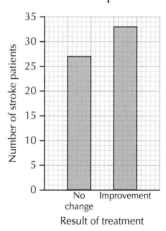

a Calculate how many more patients improved compared with those whose condition did not change.

b Calculate the percentage of patients who improved as a result of stem cell treatment.

6 Enzymes and their use in industry

1   **a** Enzymes are biological catalysts.

   Describe what is meant by the term **catalyst**.

   b Name the type of substance from which enzymes are made.

2   The list shows words related to enzyme reactions.

   specific   substrate   product   unchanged

   Copy and complete the following table using words from the list.

Word	Meaning
	the substance made after an enzyme reaction
	enzymes work on only one type of substance
	the substance on which an enzyme works
	the effect of a reaction on an enzyme

3   Copy the table. Decide if each statement about enzymes is TRUE or FALSE then tick (✓) the correct box.

   If the statement is FALSE, write the correct word(s) in the Correction box to replace the word(s) <u>underlined</u> in the statement.

Statement	True	False	Correction
Enzymes are <u>unchanged</u> by the chemical reactions they catalyse.			
Enzymes <u>slow down</u> chemical reactions.			
Enzyme action is <u>non-specific</u>.			

4   The diagram shows an experiment set up to compare the effects of biological and non-biological washing powder on grass stains.

   Identify **two** variables that must be kept the same for beaker **A** and **B** so that a valid conclusion can be drawn from the results.

   Hint   For more information on how to plan experiments see page vii.

5 The diagram shows a beaker set up to investigate the effect of temperature on the action of a biological washing powder.

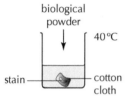

Describe how another beaker should be set up to investigate a lower temperature.

6 The diagram shows a test tube set up to investigate the effect of pH on the breakdown of starch by the enzyme amylase.

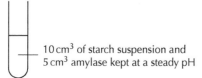

10 cm³ of starch suspension and
5 cm³ amylase kept at a steady pH

The experiment was repeated at different pH levels and the percentage of the starch broken down in 10 minutes was recorded as shown in the table.

pH	% of starch broken down in 10 minutes
3	0
4	10
5	64
6	100
7	46
8	24
9	6
10	0

a Copy and complete the line graph to show the effect of pH on the breakdown of starch by amylase.

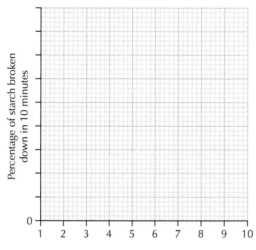

b Identify the pH at which amylase is most active.

7 The diagram shows an experiment that was set up to identify the enzyme which can break down protein. Four different enzymes were placed in holes in a dish of cloudy protein jelly. The cloudy jelly turns clear when its protein is broken down.

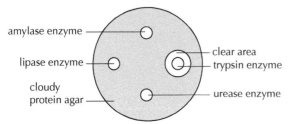

amylase enzyme

lipase enzyme

cloudy protein agar

clear area
trypsin enzyme

urease enzyme

a It was concluded that only the trypsin enzyme broke down the protein.

Explain how the conclusion was reached.

b The experiment was repeated four times using only trypsin.

The results are shown in the table.

Dish	Diameter of clear area (mm) around trypsin enzyme
1	4·7
2	3·9
3	4·2
4	4·4

Calculate the average diameter of the clear areas around the trypsin.

> Hint For more information on how to calculate an average see page vi.

8 A student carried out an investigation to compare the effectiveness of detergents on stain removal. He used two types of detergents on two different materials at two different temperatures.

His results are shown in the table.

Type of detergent	T-shirt material	Temperature (°C)	Stain remaining (%)
biological	cotton	30	7
non-biological	cotton	30	22
biological	nylon	40	0
non-biological	nylon	40	15

a Identify the type of detergent, T-shirt material and temperature which left the T-shirt with **most** stain remaining.

b Calculate the percentage of stain removed by the biological detergent from the cotton T-shirt at 30 °C.

c The student concluded that non-biological washing powder works best at 40 °C.

Explain why this is **not** a valid conclusion from these results.

d Give **one** valid conclusion that can be drawn about the effectiveness of biological detergents from this investigation.

7 Microorganisms

1 The diagrams show cells of two different microorganisms.

fungal cell

bacterium

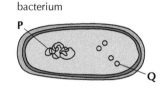

a Name a structure visible in the fungal cell which shows that it is **not** a bacterium.

b Name structures **P** and **Q** in the bacterium and the substance from which they are made.

2 A student carried out an experiment to show the effect of temperature on the growth of yeast cells. Samples of yeast cells in $5\,mm^3$ of sugar solution were placed on microscope slides and the numbers of cells present were counted. After 2 hours at different temperatures, the numbers of cells present were counted again.

The results are shown in the table.

Temperature (°C)	Number of yeast cells in sample at start	Number of yeast cells in sample after 2 hours
10	50	60
20	55	100
30	50	560
40	45	140

a Calculate the increase in the number of cells present after 2 hours at 20°C.

b Calculate the average number of yeast cells in all the samples after 2 hours.

c Identify the best temperature for the growth of yeast.

3 An experiment was carried out to find how well four antifungal creams prevented yeast growth. A sample of each cream was placed on jelly which had some yeast added.

The results are shown in the diagram.

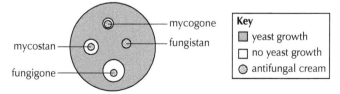

a Identify the creams which seemed best and worst at preventing yeast growth.

b Give **one** variable that should have been kept the same when carrying out this experiment.

4 An investigation was carried out to find out how the concentration of an antifungal substance affected its ability to kill fungus.

Some of the results are shown in the bar chart.

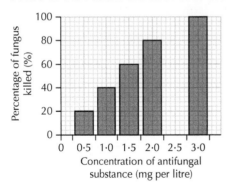

Concentration of antifungal substance (mg per litre)

a Describe how the concentration of the antifungal substance affects its ability to kill fungus.

b Identify the percentage of fungus killed by the 1.0 mg per litre concentration.

c Predict the percentage of fungus that would have been killed by the 2·5 mg per litre concentration.

> Hint For more information on how to make a prediction using a bar chart see page viii.

5 An experiment to test how well antibiotics prevented bacterial growth was carried out.

A liquid containing one species of bacteria was spread over the agar jelly.

Round paper discs, each soaked with one of the antibiotics A–F, were placed on agar jelly in a dish and left in a warm place for 5 days.

The results are shown in the diagram.

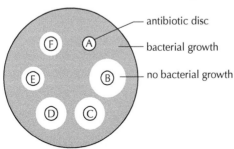

a It was concluded that antibiotic A could not prevent growth of any bacteria.

Explain why this conclusion is **not** valid.

b Identify the antibiotic which prevented most growth of the species of bacteria used.

6 Four different antibacterial cleaners **P, Q, R** and **S** were tested to find their effects on bacteria **X** and **Y**.

A liquid containing bacteria **X** was spread across the agar gel in one Petri dish. Bacteria **Y** was spread across the agar gel in the second Petri dish. The antibacterial cleaners were then placed into holes in the agar gel as shown in the diagram. The dishes were then kept warm for 5 days.

The results are shown in the diagrams.

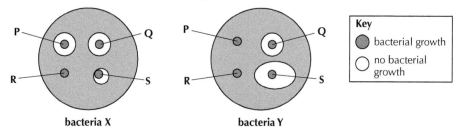

bacteria X   bacteria Y

a Identify the following antibacterial cleaners.

   i   The cleaner that is **not** effective against either of the bacteria.

   ii **Two** cleaners that are effective against both bacteria.

   iii The cleaner that is most effective against bacteria **Y**.

b Describe a control for this experiment which would prove that the results obtained were due to the effects of the cleaners and not some other factor.

> **Hint**   For more information on experimental controls see page vii.

7 The line graph shows the number of living yeast cells in a fermenter over a period of 24 hours at 20 °C.

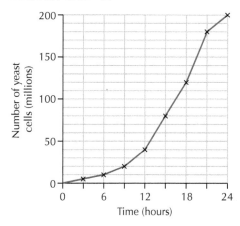

a State the number of living yeast cells present at 18 hours.

b State the time at which there were 10 million cells present.

c Predict the effect on yeast growth of raising the temperature in the fermenter to 30 °C.

8 Microorganisms in industry

1 Describe **two** properties of microorganisms that have made them useful in industry.

2 The grid shows words related to microorganisms in industry.

A carbon dioxide	B lactic acid	C ethanol
D sugar	E yeast	F bacteria

Choose **one** letter from the grid to identify the following:

a Microorganism used in the brewing of beer

b Forms bubbles in dough during baking

c Causes thickening of milk in yoghurt making

d Type of alcohol made during brewing

e Food for microorganisms used in industry

f Microorganism added to milk to make cheese

3 The list shows foods produced using microorganisms.

> **yoghurt   beer   cheese   bread**

a Identify **two** products that are made using yeast.

b Identify **two** products that are made using bacteria.

4 The fermenter shown in the diagram can be used to grow yeast in industry.

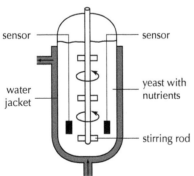

a The nutrient levels in the solution must be controlled.

   Give **two** other conditions that must be controlled and could be monitored by the sensors.

b Name **one** nutrient which is added to yeast to supply it with energy.

c Suggest why the fermenter is fitted with a stirring rod.

5 The graph shows how the pH of milk changed during the industrial production of yoghurt.

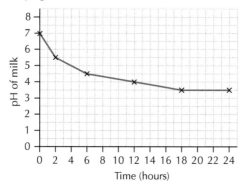

a State what is measured on the pH scale.

b Identify the hour at which the pH:

  i reached 4·0

  ii first reached its lowest value.

c Identify the pH at hour 6.

d Calculate the decrease in pH over the 24 hours.

> **Hint** For more on how to select information from a line graph see page v.

6 The diagram shows a fermenter being used in industry.

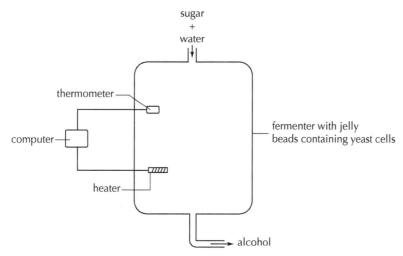

a The computer is being used to monitor and control:

  A sugar

  B yeast

  C alcohol

  D temperature.

b The fermenter was also supplied with oxygen. The scale shows oxygen delivery to the fermenter each minute.

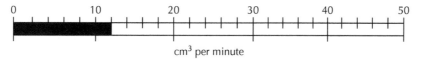

  i Calculate how much oxygen would be delivered in 1 hour.

  ii Calculate how long it would take to deliver 240 cm³ of oxygen to the fermenter.

7 Microorganisms are used in the antibiotic industry. They are grown in fermenters as shown in the diagram.

The volume of a fermenter was 1000 litres.

If the microorganism produced 10 g of antibiotic per litre per day, calculate the mass of antibiotic that was produced after:

a 1 day

b 1 week.

antibiotic

8 The diagram shows fermenters set up to monitor the growth of four different species of bacteria in identical conditions.

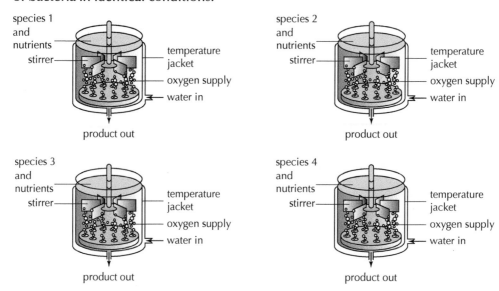

a Identify the variable that was being investigated in this experiment.

b Identify **two** variables which should have been kept constant for each fermenter.

c Suggest how the amount of product could be used to give an indication of bacterial growth.

9 Photosynthesis

This exercise includes coverage of:

N3 The process of photosynthesis

CL3 Biodiversity and interdependence SCN 3-02a

1 Copy and complete the table to show the raw materials for photosynthesis and where in the environment they are found.

Raw material	Where found
	soil
carbon dioxide	

2 Name the green substance that plants need to carry out photosynthesis.

3 Name the form of energy used by producers to carry out photosynthesis.

4 Copy and complete the word equation for photosynthesis using the words from the list.

glucose   carbon dioxide   water   oxygen

_ _ _ _ _ _   _ _ _ _ _ _ _ + _ _ _ _ _ → _ _ _ _ _ _ _ + _ _ _ _ _ _

5 Name the substance that is used by plants as a store of food.

6 The apparatus in the diagram can be used to measure photosynthesis in pondweed.

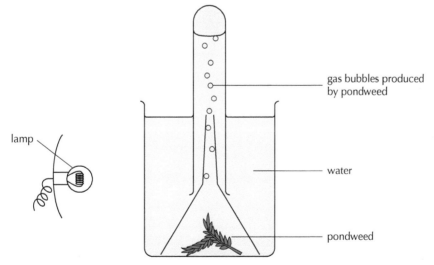

gas bubbles produced
by pondweed

lamp

water

pondweed

a Name the gas that is produced by the pondweed.

b Name the gas that is a raw material for photosynthesis and which would be dissolved in the water in the beaker.

7 Write an account of the ways in which green plants help to sustain life on Earth.

You should include at least **three** ways in your answer.

8 A de-starched plant leaf was partly covered by black card as shown in Diagram 1. It was then exposed to bright light for 24 hours. The card was removed and the leaf was tested for starch. The results are shown in Diagram 2.

Diagram 1   Diagram 2

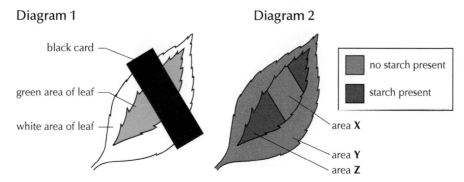

a Explain why area **X does not** have any starch after 24 hours.

b Explain why area **Y does not** have any starch after 24 hours.

c Explain why area **Z does** have starch after 24 hours.

9 The diagram shows an experiment on photosynthesis.

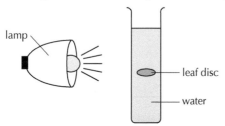

After the lamp was switched on, the leaf disc floated to the surface because oxygen gas was produced in the leaf. The time taken for this to happen was measured.
The experiment was repeated six times with different leaf discs and the results are shown in the table.

Experiment	Time for disc to reach surface (seconds)
1	18
2	17
3	12
4	15
5	12
6	16

a i Give **one** feature of the leaf discs that must be kept the same for each experiment.

ii Give **one** feature, not relating to the leaf discs, that must be kept the same for each experiment.

b Calculate the average time for the leaf discs to reach the surface.

c Bringing the lamp closer to the leaf disc increases the intensity of the light.

Describe how this could be used to investigate the effect of light intensity on the rate of photosynthesis.

10 Four identical greenhouses were planted with equal numbers of the same variety of cucumber plants.

The mass of cucumbers produced in each greenhouse was measured and the results are shown in the table.

Greenhouse	Mass of cucumbers produced (kg)
1	120
2	90
3	110
4	100

a Calculate the average mass of cucumbers produced in the greenhouses.

b Plants need light to carry out photosynthesis.

Predict what would happen to the mass of cucumbers produced if additional lighting was provided in the greenhouses.

11 The apparatus in the diagram can be used to show that carbon dioxide is needed for photosynthesis.

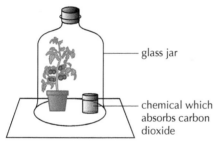
glass jar

chemical which absorbs carbon dioxide

a Which of the following set-ups, **A** to **D**, could be used as a control for this experiment?

A
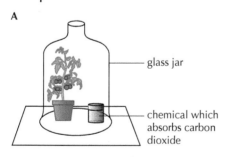
glass jar

chemical which absorbs carbon dioxide

B
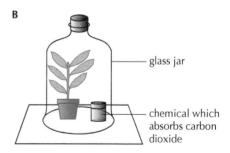
glass jar

chemical which absorbs carbon dioxide

C
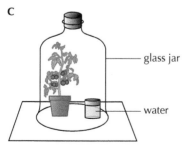
glass jar

water

D
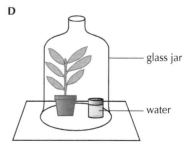
glass jar

water

b To find if photosynthesis had occurred in the plants, their leaves were tested with iodine solution.

Name the substance which is tested for with iodine solution.

10 Limiting factors in photosynthesis

This exercise includes coverage of:

N4 The effect of limiting factors in photosynthesis

1 Give **three** factors that can limit the rate of photosynthesis in green plants.

2 The apparatus shown can be used to measure the rate of photosynthesis in pondweed.

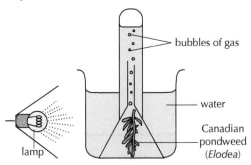

a Name the gas being released during photosynthesis.

b Name the gas dissolved in the water which could be acting as a limiting factor for photosynthesis.

c Describe how the intensity of the light could be varied using this apparatus.

3 The graph shows the effect of increasing carbon dioxide concentration on the rate of photosynthesis in a green plant.

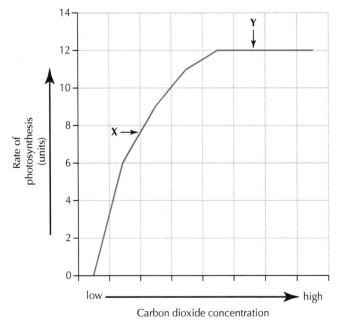

a Identify the factor that is limiting the rate of photosynthesis at point **X** on the graph.

b Give **one** factor that could be limiting the rate of photosynthesis at point **Y** on the graph.

4 The graph shows the effect of increasing light intensity on the rate of photosynthesis in a green plant at 30 °C.

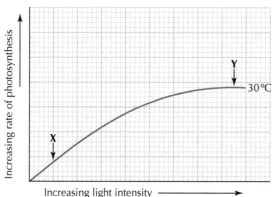

a Identify the factor that limits the rate of photosynthesis at point **X**.

b Predict the effect on the rate of photosynthesis at point **Y** if the temperature were changed to 20 °C.

5 The rate of photosynthesis was measured in a tomato plant at different temperatures. At each temperature tested, the light intensity and carbon dioxide concentration supplied to the plant were kept the same.

The results are shown in the table.

Temperature (°C)	Rate of photosynthesis (cm³ of oxygen produced per minute)
5	3
10	6
15	12
20	17
25	17
30	17

a On a piece of graph paper, plot a line graph to show the results.

> Hint For more information on how to draw a line graph see page vi.

b i Give **one** conclusion that can be drawn from the results.

ii Explain why keeping the light intensity and carbon dioxide concentration the same was essential for a valid conclusion to be drawn.

11 Respiration

N4 Process of respiration

CL3 Biodiversity and interdependence SCN 4-02b

1 Copy and complete the word equation for aerobic respiration using the key words from the list.

energy   carbon dioxide   water   sugar   oxygen

_ _ _ _ _ + _ _ _ _ _ _ → _ _ _ _ _ _ + _ _ _ _ _ _   _ _ _ _ _ _ _ + _ _ _ _ _

2 The grid contains terms related to respiration in living organisms.

A water	**B** lactic acid	**C** carbon dioxide
D alcohol	**E** sugar	**F** oxygen

Choose **one** letter to identify the following substances.

a The gas needed for aerobic respiration

b Energy is released from this substance during respiration

c Produced in both aerobic respiration and fermentation in yeast

d Commercial product when yeast respires without oxygen in brewing

e Produced when animal cells respire without oxygen

f The liquid produced when animal cells respire aerobically

3 Describe **one** advantage to a living cell of respiring with oxygen rather than without it.

4 The apparatus shown can be used to measure the rate of respiration in yeast.

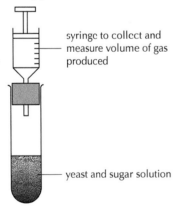

syringe to collect and measure volume of gas produced

yeast and sugar solution

a Name the gas collected in the syringe which is produced when the yeast respires without oxygen.

b Name a substance that would appear in the tube as a product of the respiration of yeast without oxygen.

5 The apparatus shown can be used to measure the effect of temperature on the volume of gas produced by respiring yeast.

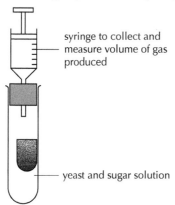

syringe to collect and measure volume of gas produced

yeast and sugar solution

The volume of gas produced at different temperatures was measured and the results are shown in the table.

	Temperature (°C)			
	15	20	25	30
Volume of gas produced (cm³)	5	14	23	32

a Copy and complete the line graph to show the results in the table.

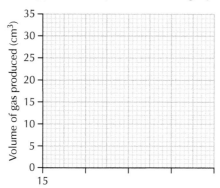

> **Hint** Remember to choose an appropriate scale and to label the horizontal axis correctly.

b i Give **one** conclusion about the effect of temperature on respiration.

> **Hint** For more information on how to draw a conclusion from a line graph see page viii.

ii Suggest why respiration is affected by changes in temperature.

6 The apparatus shown can be used to demonstrate that sugar is needed for respiration.

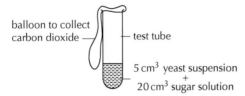

balloon to collect carbon dioxide — test tube

5 cm³ yeast suspension + 20 cm³ sugar solution

Which of the following, **A** to **D**, could be used as a control for the above experiment?

A

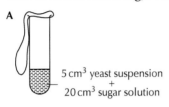

5 cm³ yeast suspension + 20 cm³ sugar solution

B

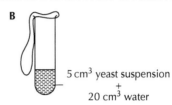

5 cm³ yeast suspension + 20 cm³ water

C

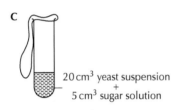

20 cm³ yeast suspension + 5 cm³ sugar solution

D

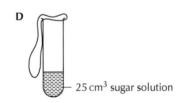

25 cm³ sugar solution

7 The diagram shows the apparatus used to investigate the rising of dough.

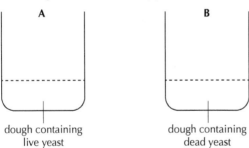

dough containing live yeast

dough containing dead yeast

The volume of dough in the beaker was measured before and after leaving it in a warm place for 6 hours.

The results are shown in the table.

Beaker	Volume of dough (cm³)	
	At start	At end
A	100	250
B	100	100

a The dough increases in volume because of carbon dioxide gas that is produced.

Calculate the increase in the volume of the dough in beaker **A**.

b Give **one** factor that would have to be kept the same so that a valid conclusion can be drawn in this investigation.

8 The apparatus shown in the diagram was set up to investigate how the variety of yeast affected alcohol production. Identical tubes were set up for each of four different yeast varieties and kept in ideal conditions for 3 days.

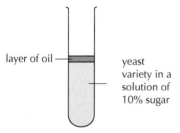

layer of oil — yeast variety in a solution of 10% sugar

At the end of the time, the percentage of alcohol in each tube was measured. The results are shown in the table.

Yeast variety	Percentage alcohol after 3 days
1	2·4
2	3·4
3	4·0
4	3·0

a Copy and complete the bar chart to show the results.

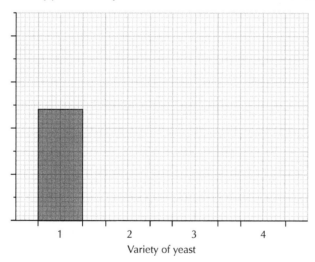

Variety of yeast

Hint   For more information on how to present information see page vi.

b Give **one** conclusion which can be drawn from the results.

c Suggest **one** factor that would need to be controlled to give 'ideal conditions' for yeast respiration.

12 Controversial biological procedures

N4 Cell biology

CL3 Body systems and cells SCN 4-13c

This list shows a number of controversial biological procedures:

- saviour siblings
- gene therapy
- pharming
- transgenic organisms
- stem cell technology
- DNA profiling

For each procedure, identify:

a **one** reason why it is undertaken

b **one** issue that makes the procedure controversial.

This goat produces a human protein in its milk that can be used to prevent uncontrolled blood clotting.

The transgenic tomatoes on the right have a longer shelf life than the other non-transgenic ones.

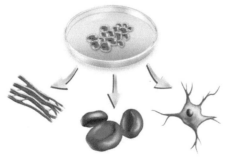

Stems cells have the power to replace damaged or diseased cells and there is hope that they may offer treatments for conditions such as Alzheimer's and Parkinson's disease.

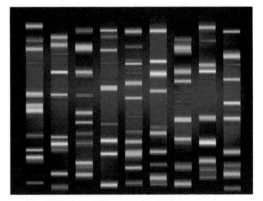

A set of DNA profiles, each unique to an individual.

13 Body systems

This exercise includes coverage of:

N3 Structure and functions of organs and organ systems

CL3 Body systems and cells SCN 3-12a

1 The human heart contracts to pump blood around the body.

Which statement is correct?

The heart is an example of:

A a cell

B an organ

C an organ system

D a tissue.

2 The diagram shows the heart, some blood vessels and the outlines of other structures in the human body.

The heart and blood vessels shown make up:

A a tissue

B an organ

C a system

D an organism.

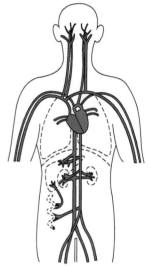

3 The diagram shows the direction of blood flowing through the blood vessels that transport blood into and out of the human heart.

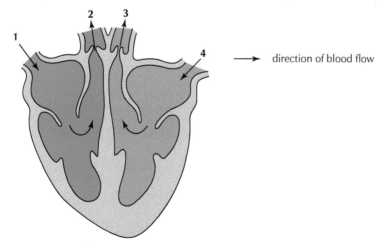

direction of blood flow

Deoxygenated blood is transported in blood vessels:

A 1 and 2   **B** 2 and 3   **C** 3 and 4   **D** 1 and 4.

4 The diagram shows part of the human respiratory system.

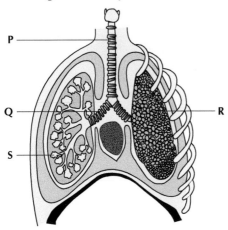

P

Q   R

S

a Name structures **P**, **Q**, **R** and **S**.

b Describe what happens to gases in structure **S**.

5 The diagram shows part of the human digestive system.

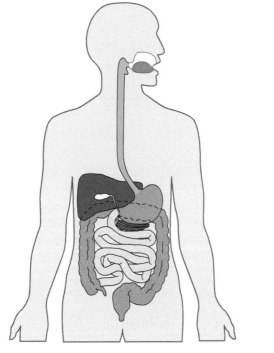

rectum

stomach

large intestine

small intestine

gullet

anus

a Arrange the structures provided in the list in the correct order to show the passage of food through the digestive system from the mouth to the anus.

b Describe what happens to food in the process of digestion.

c State the function of the small intestine.

6 The graph shows the pulse rate of two students before, during and after exercise.

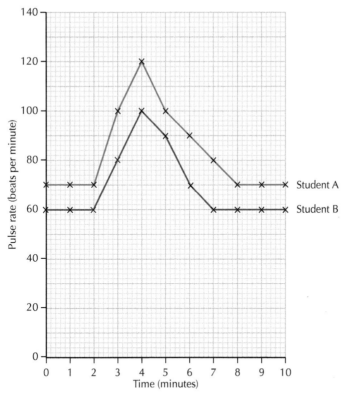

a During which time period were the students exercising?

    A 0–2 minutes

    B 0–4 minutes

    C 2–4 minutes

    D 2–8 minutes

b Give the resting pulse rate of Student A.

c Give **one** variable that should have been kept the same to allow a valid comparison to be made between the students' pulse rates.

d Use information in the graph to identify the fitter student and give a reason to support your answer.

7 **a** The table shows the responses of a group of 160 15-year-olds living in Scotland when asked about their smoking habits.

	Responses			
	Never smoked	Tried smoking but stopped	Occasional smoker	Regular smoker
Percentage of 15-year-olds	50	25	12·5	12·5

This information is presented in the pie chart.

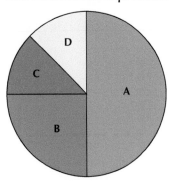

  i Identify the part of the pie chart that represents the percentage of 15-year-olds who tried smoking but stopped.

  ii Calculate the number of students in the sample who are regular smokers.

b The table shows the results of a survey into smoking and pregnancy.

Smoking habit of mothers during pregnancy	Average mass of babies at birth (kg)
non-smoker	3·40
light smoker	3·20
heavy smoker	3·18

  i Describe how smoking by mothers during pregnancy affected the average mass of their babies at birth.

  ii Explain why the figures for non-smokers were included in the survey.

14 Role of technology in monitoring health

This exercise includes coverage of:

N3 The role of technology in monitoring health and improving quality of life

CL3 Body systems and cells SCN 3-12b

1 The diagram shows the health triangle.

  a Give **one** example of activity that would contribute to the social aspect of health.

  b Give the aspects of health shown on the triangle diagram at **X** and **Y**.

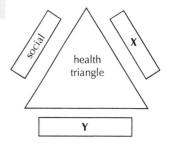

2 Smoking cigarettes can increase the risk of:

  A diabetes   **B** anorexia

  C cancer   **D** arthritis.

3 The following list refers to medical conditions.

    1 asthma

    2 type 2 diabetes

    3 high blood pressure

  Being overweight can lead to an increased risk of conditions:

  A 1 and 2 only   **B** 1 and 3 only

  C 2 and 3 only   **D** 1, 2 and 3.

4 The diagram shows an instrument that is used to measure blood pressure.

  This instrument is called a:

  A pulsometer   **B** stethoscope

  C digital heart rate monitor   **D** digital sphygmomanometer.

5 Which instrument is used to measure lung fitness?

  A glucometer   **B** sphygmomanometer

  C peak-flow meter   **D** pulsometer

6 High blood pressure can lead to:

  A angina and heart attack   **B** stroke and obesity

  C obesity and heart attack   **D** stroke and diabetes.

7 Peak flow can be used in the diagnosis and management of:

  A asthma   **B** diabetes

  C heart disease   **D** leukaemia.

8 The table shows the number of people in a family with four different health conditions.

Health condition	Number of people
angina	5
high blood pressure	10
low blood pressure	2
had a stroke	3

Calculate the simplest whole number ratio of people with high blood pressure compared to those with low blood pressure.

Hint For more information on how to calculate a ratio see page vi.

9 **a** Three peak-flow readings of a 14-year-old student were taken using a peak-flow meter, shown on the right.

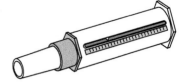

Reading	Peak flow (litres per minute)
1	500
2	510
3	490

Calculate the student's average peak-flow rate.

Hint For more information on how to calculate an average see page vi.

b The grid contains information about six students who took part in an investigation about peak flow.

A	B	C
Fit male	Fit male	Fit male
Age 15	Age 15	Age 30
Mass 60 kg	Mass 65 kg	Mass 60 kg
D	**E**	**F**
Fit female	Fit female	Unfit female
Age 30	Age 15	Age 30
Mass 60 kg	Mass 50 kg	Mass 50 kg

i State which **two** students should be compared to investigate the effect of age on peak flow.

ii State **one** factor which could be investigated if **C** and **D** were compared.

10 a A person's resting pulse rate can be used as a guide to their level of fitness, as shown in the table.

Resting pulse rate (beats per minute)	Level of fitness
below 50	outstanding
50–60	good
61–90	normal
above 90	poor

Identify the level of fitness of a person with a resting pulse rate of 48 beats per minute.

b Some students measured their resting pulse rate to estimate their level of fitness.

The results are shown in the table.

Level of fitness	Number of students
outstanding	1
good	7
normal	10
poor	2
	total = 20

On a piece of grid paper, copy and complete the bar chart by:

1 copying the horizontal axis label as shown

2 adding a label and scale on the vertical axis

3 drawing the bars.

Hint For more information on how to present information see page vi.

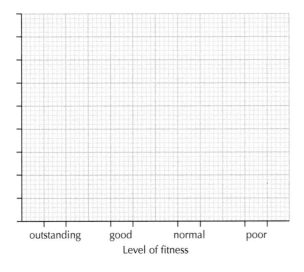

15 Body defences against disease and the role of vaccines

1. Give **one** example of a first-line defence barrier in the human body.

2. Give the name of the body system that helps fight off infection.

3. State what happens to the number of white blood cells in a person with an infection.

4. The diagram shows a white blood cell and a disease-causing microorganism.

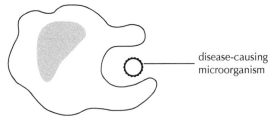

disease-causing microorganism

   Describe the action of this white blood cell.

5. One type of white blood cell produces antibodies.
   Describe the role of antibodies.

6. Give **one** example of a type of microorganism that can cause disease.

7. Give the term used to describe disease caused by microorganisms.

8. Name the chemicals produced by some white blood cells that attach to microorganisms and destroy them.

9. What name is given to the chemicals produced by the body in response to a vaccine?

   A antibiotics

   B antibodies

   C hormones

   D enzymes

10. Elderly people and those with asthma are advised to be vaccinated against flu.

    a Describe **one** benefit of having this vaccination to the individual.

    b Suggest **one** benefit to the health service **or** other people in the community.

11. Give an example of **one** physical and **one** chemical first-line defence barrier in the human body that can help to prevent infection by microorganisms.

12 Copy and complete the sentences using the correct terms from the following list.

> antibodies   microorganisms   tear fluid   stomach acid
> bacteria   infections   viruses

Diseases caused by microorganisms are called _ _ _ _ _ _ _ _ _ _.

Most infections are caused by _ _ _ _ _ _ _ _ and _ _ _ _ _ _ _.

First-line defence barriers include _ _ _ _ _ _ _ _ _ _ _ and _ _ _ _ _ _ _ _ _.

13 The following list gives some examples of the body's defences against disease.

> skin   mucus   antibodies   stomach acid   tear fluid

Use the words in the list to answer the following questions.

a Give **two** examples of first-line defence barriers.

b Copy and complete the following sentences.

 i _ _ _ _ _ _ _ _ _ contains enzymes that destroy microorganisms landing on the surface of the eye.

 ii _ _ _ _ _ is a sticky substance that traps microorganisms and prevents them passing into the lungs.

 iii _ _ _ _ _ _ _ _ _ _ _ kills microorganisms that are swallowed.

c Name the chemicals produced by white blood cells that attach to microorganisms and destroy them.

14 Vaccinations are given to provide immunity against some diseases.

a Explain what is meant by **immunity**.

b Give **one** example of a disease that we can be vaccinated against.

15 Read the short summary of Edward Jenner's work on vaccines.

> Jenner collected pus containing cowpox virus from the hand of a milkmaid.
>
> Jenner then infected an 8-year-old boy called James Phipps with the cowpox virus. Over the following days, James developed a fever, but soon became well again. Two weeks later, Jenner injected the dangerous smallpox virus into James. Fortunately, James did not develop smallpox.

Copy and complete the sentences using words from the list to make the sentences about the passage correct.

> antibiotics   sensitive   antibodies   infection   immune

a The cowpox virus from the milkmaid caused James to become _ _ _ _ _ _ to the smallpox virus.

b James' body had produced _ _ _ _ _ _ _ _ _ _ which stopped the smallpox virus from causing an infection.

16 Concerns have been raised that doctors' clothing might transmit bacteria from one patient to another. An investigation in a hospital showed that 50% of the neckties worn by doctors had disease-causing bacteria on them. However, only 10% of the ties worn by a control group of security staff at the hospital had disease-causing bacteria on them.

Suggest why ties worn by the security staff at the hospital were chosen as the control group to make a comparison.

17 Read the following passage and use the information to answer the questions.

Whooping cough immunisation started in 1951 in the UK and led to a sharp fall in the number of child deaths caused by this disease. However, in 1974, a report suggested a link between whooping cough immunisation and brain damage in some children. As a result, by 1978, the percentage of children being immunised decreased to only 30%. This led to large outbreaks of whooping cough in 1978 and 1982. Later research showed no link between whooping cough immunisation and brain damage. Immunisation uptake increased again and, by the late 1990s, 94% of children in the UK were being immunised.

a Give the year when whooping cough immunisation started in the UK.

b Explain why only 30% of children were immunised against whooping cough in 1978.

c Give the percentage of children who were **not** being immunised against whooping cough by the late 1990s.

18 Immunity against polio can be given by vaccinations.

The first vaccination is given at the age of 3 months and it is followed by two 'boosters'.

The graph gives information about these vaccinations.

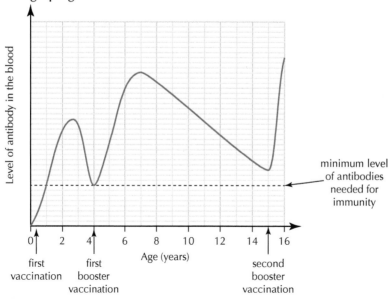

a Identify the age at which the minimum level of antibodies needed for immunity was first reached.

b Calculate how many years after the first booster vaccination the second booster vaccination was given.

c Suggest why booster vaccinations are needed.

16 Fertilisation and embryonic development

1 The diagrams represent parts of the human male and female reproductive systems.

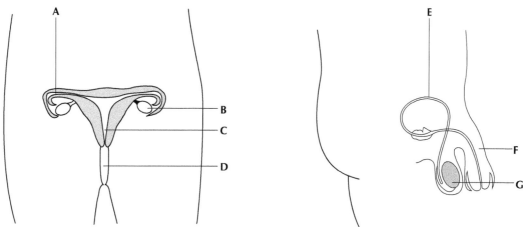

Copy and complete the table by adding the correct letters, names and functions of the labelled structures.

Letter	Name	Function
A		site of fertilisation
F		deposits sperm
B	ovary	
G	testis	
	uterus	development of embryo

2 Use words from the list to copy and complete the following sentences. Each word can be used once, more than once or not at all.

> foetus   nucleus   uterus   embryo

a Fertilisation occurs when the _ _ _ _ _ _ _ of a sperm cell fuses with the _ _ _ _ _ _ _ of an egg cell.

b A fertilised egg divides repeatedly to form a ball of cells called an _ _ _ _ _ _.

c The _ _ _ _ _ _ is the part of the female reproductive system where the embryo develops.

d The _ _ _ _ _ _ is the name given to the later stages of development when the organs of the embryo have developed.

3 The diagram shows a foetus during its later stages of development in the uterus.

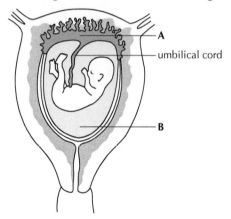

A

umbilical cord

B

a i Name part **A**.

  ii Name **one** useful substance that moves through part **A** from the mother to the embryo.

  iii Name the waste gas that passes across part **A** from the embryo to the mother.

  iv Name **one** virus that can cross part **A** and harm the developing embryo.

  v Name **one** harmful substance that can cross part **A** and affect the development of the embryo.

b i Name part **B**.

  ii State the function of part **B**.

c Describe the function of the umbilical cord.

4 The average production of sperm cells by a bull throughout the first six months of the year is shown in the table.

Month	Average sperm production (millions of cells per day)
January	14 000
February	13 500
March	13 000
April	12 500
May	12 000
June	11 000

a Describe how sperm production changes between January and June.

b From the results, suggest **one** environmental factor which affects sperm cell production.

c In May, bulls produce a daily average of 8 cm³ of fluid that contains sperm cells.

  Calculate how many sperm cells would be contained in 1 cm³ of this fluid.

N4 Sexual and asexual reproduction and their importance for survival of species

CL4 Body systems and cells SCN 4-14b

1 **a** Sexual reproduction involves gametes.

The following diagrams represent human gametes.

5 micrometres

100 micrometres

A   B

   i   Name gametes **A** and **B**.

   ii Other than size, describe **one** difference between the gametes.

   iii Explain the advantage to cell **A** of being very small and the advantage to cell **B** of being larger.

b In flowering plants, the gametes are produced inside the flowers.

The diagram shows a grass flower.

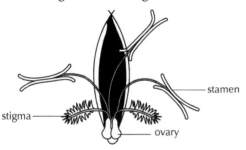

stamen

stigma

ovary

   i   Name the male gametes produced by the stamens.

   ii Name the structure that contains the female gamete.

c Describe what happens during fertilisation.

d The offspring produced by sexual reproduction show differences from each other.

Explain why variation is important to a species.

2 Copy and complete the following sentences by selecting the correct words from the choice brackets.

a Sexual reproduction involves the fusion of (**testes / gametes**) and usually involves (**one / two**) parent(s).

b In fish and amphibians, fertilisation is (**internal / external**). To help ensure fertilisation and survival of the species (**many / few**) eggs and sperm are released.

c In reptiles, birds and mammals, fertilisation is (**internal / external**). This method makes fertilisation more likely and so (**fewer / more**) eggs and sperm are needed.

3 Some unicellular organisms reproduce by cell division. This is an example of asexual reproduction.

a Give the meaning of **asexual reproduction**.

b Give **one** example of a microorganism that reproduces by asexual reproduction.

c Give **one** advantage and **one** disadvantage to an organism of reproducing asexually.

d Give **one** method of asexual reproduction used by flowering plants.

e Copy and complete the following sentence by selecting the correct words from the choice brackets.

Asexual reproduction of certain plants is an (**advantage** / **disadvantage**) to garden centres as this enables them to sell plants with the (**same** / **different**) characteristics all year round.

4 Many plants reproduce asexually.

The diagrams show two natural methods of asexual reproduction in flowering plants.

A

strawberry plant

B

potato plant

a Name the examples of asexual reproduction shown in **A** and **B**.

b Give **one** advantage of asexual reproduction to plants.

c Describe **one** feature of asexual reproduction.

d Give the term used to describe genetically identical organisms produced from one parent.

5 Sticklebacks build nests in which eggs are released and fertilised.

A survey was carried out to estimate the number of sticklebacks by counting the nests in five separate areas of the loch.

The results are shown in the table.

Area	Number of nests
1	6
2	12
3	9
4	11
5	7

a Calculate the average number of nests found in the five areas.

b If each nest represents a pair of sticklebacks, estimate the total number of sticklebacks in the five areas.

c On a piece of graph paper, draw a bar chart to show the results of the survey.

18 Propagating and growing plants

This exercise includes coverage of:

N4 Propagating and growing plants

CL4 Biodiversity and interdependence SCN 4-02a

1 A bean seed is shown in the diagram.

Copy and complete the table by inserting the names and functions of the parts of the bean seed.

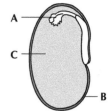

Part	Name	Description of function
A		grows into the new plant
B	seed coat	
C		provides food for growth

2 The diagrams show two natural methods of asexual reproduction in flowering plants.

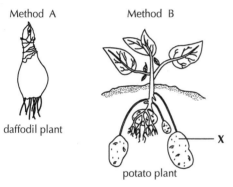

Method A

daffodil plant

Method B

potato plant

X

a Name the **two** methods of asexual reproduction.

b Explain how structure **X** contributes to the growth of a new potato plant.

c Give **two** advantages of propagating plants by asexual methods.

d Name **one** artificial method of propagating flowering plants.

3 The root length of a germinating kidney bean seedling was measured every 2 days.

The results are shown in the table.

Time (days)	Root length (mm)
0	0
2	4
4	8
6	18
8	27

a Copy and complete the line graph by:

i   providing a label for the horizontal axis

ii completing the scale on the vertical axis

iii plotting the results.

b Identify the **two** days in which the greatest increase in root length occurred.

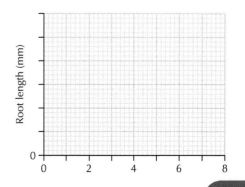

4 An investigation into the conditions required for germination was carried out as shown in the diagram.

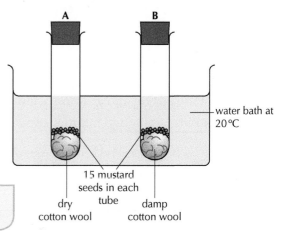

water bath at 20°C

15 mustard seeds in each tube

dry cotton wool   damp cotton wool

a Give the variable that was being investigated.

b Results show that 12 of the 15 seeds sown in tube **B** germinated.

Calculate the percentage germination in this tube.

Hint For more information on how to calculate a percentage see page vi.

c Predict the effect on the number of seeds germinating if the investigation was repeated at 0°C.

5 Six pots were set up to investigate the growth of hyacinth and crocus bulbs.

The time taken for the shoots to appear was measured.

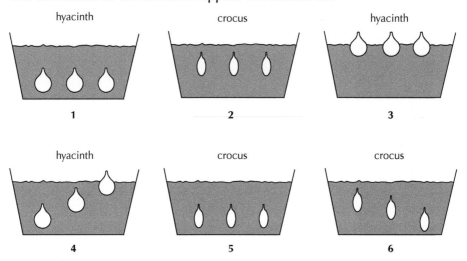

hyacinth   crocus   hyacinth

1   2   3

hyacinth   crocus   crocus

4   5   6

a Identify the **two** pots which should be compared to investigate the effect of depth of planting on the growth of crocus bulbs.

Hint For more information on experimental controls see page vii.

b Give **one** variable that should be kept the same to allow a valid conclusion to be made.

c State what could be done to increase the reliability of the results.

Hint For more information on how to improve reliability in an experiment see page viii.

6 The table shows the mass of sugar present in one food storage organ of two plants, **X** and **Y**.

Plant	Mass of sugar per food storage organ (g)
X	54
Y	6

Calculate the number of food storage organs of plant **Y** needed to give the same mass of sugar as one food storage organ of plant **X**.

7 The effect of temperature on the germination of oat seeds and barley seeds is shown in the graph.

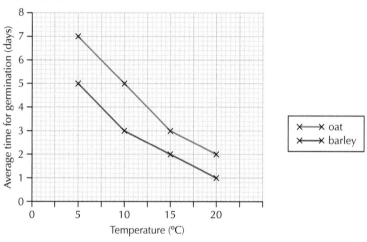

a Describe the effect of increasing temperature on the average time for germination in both seeds.

> **Hint** For more information on how to draw a conclusion from a line graph see page viii.

b Give the average time for oat seeds to germinate at 5 °C.

c Calculate the difference in the average time taken for barley seeds to germinate at 5 °C and 20 °C.

> **Hint** For more on how to select information from a line graph see page v.

19 Commercial use of plants

This exercise includes coverage of:
N4 Commercial use of plants
CL4 Biodiversity and interdependence SCN 4-02a

1 Give **two** commercial uses of plants.

2 Give **one** example of the use of plants for aesthetic reasons.

3 Name the process by which plants are genetically modified to produce medicines.

4 Explain what is meant by **pharming**.

5 Give **one** advantage of producing medicines by pharming.

6 Give **one** disadvantage of using genetically modified plants to produce medicines.

7 The list shows plants that are grown commercially.

> soya bean   spruce tree   cotton   oak tree   poppy
>
> wheat   maize   rose

a Which **two** plants can be used for building materials?

b Which plant is used to produce a painkilling medicine?

c Which plant produces fibres that can be used for clothing?

d Which **three** plants are widely used for food?

8 The chart shows the times when different vegetable crops can be sown and harvested for food.

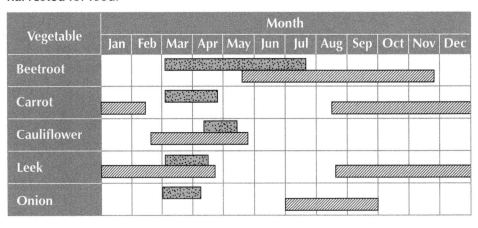

Vegetable	Month											
	Jan	Feb	Mar	Apr	May	Jun	Jul	Aug	Sep	Oct	Nov	Dec
Beetroot			sowing					harvesting				
Carrot	harvesting		sowing						harvesting			
Cauliflower			harvesting	sowing								
Leek	harvesting		sowing						harvesting			
Onion			sowing			harvesting						

sowing times   harvesting times

a Give the month in which it is possible to sow seeds of all the vegetables.

b State which crop can be harvested over the longest period of time.

c Name **all** the crops that can be harvested in the same month as seeds of the same species are being sown.

9 The diagrams show features of some newly discovered plants.

scented flowers with brightly coloured petals

Plant **A**

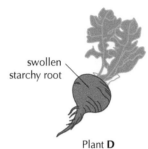

tough stem with strong fibres

Plant **B**

pods with bitter tasting seeds

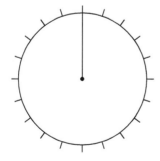

Plant **C**

swollen starchy root

Plant **D**

The following list provides some possible uses for the plants shown in the diagrams.

raw material   perfume   medicine   food   aesthetic   decorative

Suggest a possible use for each plant feature.

10 The table shows the area of an agricultural region used to grow five main food crops as a percentage of the total.

Crop	Area of land used (%)
oats	5
potatoes	5
oil seed rape	10
wheat	25
barley	55

a Use the information from the table to copy and complete a pie chart as shown.

b If 10 000 hectares of land is available to grow crops, calculate the area of land used for oil seed rape.

c Calculate the simplest whole-number ratio of the area of the land used to grow barley to the area of land used to grow potatoes.

20 Genetic information and inheritance

This exercise includes coverage of:

N4 Genetic information

CL4 Inheritance SCN 4-14c

 1 Choose terms from the list to match the descriptions.

> phenotype   genotype   alleles   homozygous   heterozygous
>
> monohybrid   dominant   recessive

a Different forms of a gene

b The form of a gene that is expressed in the phenotype, whether homozygous or heterozygous

c The alleles that an organism has for a particular characteristic

d A genotype in which the two alleles for the characteristic are different

e A genotype in which the two alleles for the characteristic are the same

f The visible characteristics of an organism that occur as a result of its genes

g Allele of a gene that only shows in the phenotype if the genotype is homozygous for that allele

h The type of cross set up to study the inheritance of contrasting characteristics caused by alleles of the same gene

2 Give the symbols used to represent the following generations:

a the parent generation of a cross

b the first generation of a cross

c the second generation of a cross.

3 State the expected phenotype ratio from a monohybrid cross between two heterozygous parents.

4 A hairy-leafed plant is crossed with a smooth-leafed plant.

All the F_1 plants had hairy leaves.

The genotype of the F_1 plants was:

A heterozygous

B homozygous

C dominant

D recessive.

5 The diagram shows the inheritance of coat colour in mice.

	phenotype:	black mouse	×	white mouse
P				
P	genotype:	BB	×	bb
F_1	genotype:		Bb	
F_2	genotypes:	BB and Bb and bb		

Which of the following generations contain heterozygous individuals?

A P and F_1 **B** P and F_2

C F_1 and F_2 **D** P, F_1 and F_2

6 A male black mouse was crossed with a female brown mouse and all of the F₁ offspring produced were black. These mice were allowed to mate and the F₂ generation contained both black and brown mice.

This shows that the black allele is dominant because:

A only one of the original parents was black

B the male parent was black

C all of the F_1 were black

D some of the F_2 were black.

7 A homozygous dominant normal winged fruit fly was crossed with a homozygous recessive vestigial winged fly. Flies from the F_1 were allowed to mate with vestigial winged flies.

What percentage of their offspring would be expected to have normal wings?

A 25%   **B** 50%

C 75%   **D** 100%

8 Feather colour in one species of parrot is controlled by alleles of a single gene.

Blue feather colour (B) is dominant to yellow feather colour (b).

A homozygous blue male parrot was crossed with a homozygous yellow female parrot.

Give the expected genotype of all of the F_1 parrots.

9 Cheek dimples are human facial features. Their presence is controlled by alleles of a single gene.

dimple

The dominant allele (D) gives dimples and the recessive allele (d) gives no dimples.

A female with the genotype DD and a male without dimples have a child.

Give the expected phenotype of their child.

10 A cross between two true-breeding pea plants is shown in the diagram.

P   true-breeding tall   ×   true-breeding dwarf

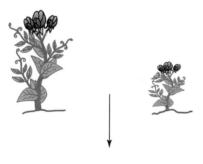

F_1 all tall

Some of the F_1 tall plants produced from the cross were bred with each other to produce a new generation of pea plants.

a Give the symbol used to identify this new generation.

b Predict the phenotype ratio which would be expected in this generation.

c Predict the genotype ratio which would be expected in this generation.

11 In mice black coat is dominant to white coat.

In a cross between heterozygous black mice and homozygous white mice, which of the following shows the predicted phenotypes of the F_1 generation?

A 3 black:1 white   B 1 black:1 white

C 1 black:3 white   D all black

12 In African leopards, the allele for spotted coat (F) is dominant to the allele for black coat (f).

Two spotted leopards produced a black offspring.

a What were the genotypes of the parents?

     A FF × ff   B FF × Ff

     C Ff × Ff   D Ff × ff

b What is the probability that another black offspring will be born to the same parents?

     A 1 in 1   B 3 in 4

     C 1 in 2   D 1 in 4

13 In guinea pigs the allele R represents rough coat and r represents smooth coat.

Two rough-coated guinea pigs were crossed and 75% of their offspring were rough coated and the remainder were smooth coated.

The parent genotypes must have been:

A RR × rr   B rr × Rr

C Rr × RR   D Rr × Rr

14 In fruit flies the allele for grey body is dominant to the allele for black body.

Two heterozygous flies were crossed and the ratio of phenotypes in the F_1 was exactly as would have been predicted. If the number of F_1 offspring was 280, what was the number of each phenotype?

A 280 grey:0 black   B 210 grey:70 black

C 140 grey:140 black   D 70 grey:210 black

15 A heterozygous, brown-eyed woman and a blue-eyed man have a child.

If the allele for brown eyes is dominant to the allele for blue eyes, what are the chances that the child is blue-eyed?

A 1 in 2   B 1 in 3

C 1 in 4   D none

16 A female fruit fly with short wings mates with a male with long wings. All the F_1 offspring are long winged.

Two of these offspring mate with each other.

What percentage of their offspring is expected to have long wings?

A 25%   B 50%

C 75%   D 100%

17 The diagram shows a maize (corn) cob with purple and yellow fruits. The cob was produced from a cross between two parent maize plants and each individual fruit represents one offspring from the cross.

Purple (P) is dominant to yellow (p). The ratio of purple fruit to yellow fruit was 3:1.

yellow fruit

purple fruit

What were the genotypes of the parent maize plants?

A PP × Pp

B PP × pp

C Pp × Pp

D pp × Pp

18 The eye colours of 120 school students are shown in the table.

Eye colour	Number of students
brown	56
green	27
blue	42
grey	16

a Calculate the percentage of students with blue eyes.

b Express the number of students with brown eyes to those with grey eyes as a simple whole number ratio.

> Hint For more information on how to calculate a ratio see page vi.

19 The results of a school survey on eye colour showed that out of 800 students, 80% had brown eyes, 10% had blue eyes and 10% had green or grey eyes.

a Calculate the number of children with green or grey eyes.

b On a separate piece of graph paper, draw a bar chart to show the percentages of students with the different eye colours.

> Hint For more information on how to present information see page vi.

21 Growth and development

1 Copy and complete the sentences using the terms provided to describe the life cycle of an annual plant.

seeds   fertilisation   germinate   fruits   pollination

Annual plant seeds _ _ _ _ _ _ _ _ and produce seedlings that grow and develop into mature plants. The mature plants flower. After _ _ _ _ _ _ _ _ _ _ _ and _ _ _ _ _ _ _ _ _ _ _ _ _, the flowers develop into _ _ _ _ _ _. The fruits contain _ _ _ _ _ which germinate the following year.

2 The graph shows the changes in the average dry mass of a broad bean plant over a growing season from seed to maturity.

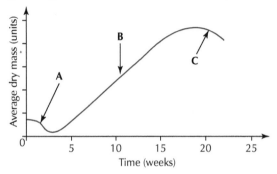

a Name the process responsible for the loss of mass in the seed at point **A** on the graph.

b Name the process responsible for the growth and gain of mass at point **B** on the graph.

c Explain the loss of mass in the plant at point **C** on the graph.

3 Make a flow chart with arrows to show the life cycle of a human by copying and arranging the following words and statements.

- Baby born 9 months after fertilisation
- Adults
- Following puberty adolescents can produce gametes
- Children grow and develop
- Male gamete fertilises female gamete

4 The graph shows the human growth curve.

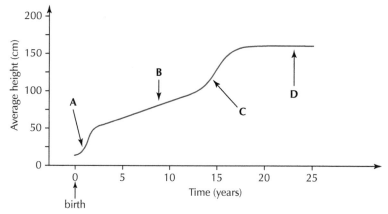

a Which letter on the graph shows the adolescent growth spurt?

b Which letter represents the full adult height?

5 Which of the following factors are all required for seed germination?

A light, water and oxygen

B water, suitable temperature and light

C light, suitable temperature and oxygen

D water, oxygen and suitable temperature

6 A variety of food groups are needed for a healthy diet.

Copy and complete the table to show the three main food groups and their uses.

Food group	Use
	energy
	growth and repair of cells and tissues
fat	

7 The bar chart shows the effect of adding different amounts of nitrogen fertiliser to the yield of barley grain in three different field trials.

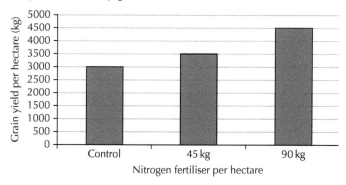

a Calculate how much more barley was harvested from a field given 90 kg per hectare than was harvested from the control.

b Give **one** conclusion about the effect of nitrogen fertiliser on the yield of barley.

c State the difference between the control barley sample and the other field trials.

d Give **two** variables that should be kept the same to allow a fair comparison between the trials to be made.

21 Growth and development   55

8 The bar chart shows the results of exposure to gamma radiation on the percentage germination success of barley seeds.

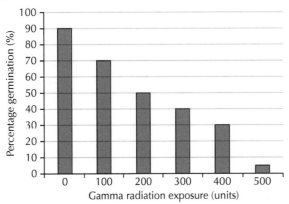

a Describe the effect of gamma radiation exposure on the percentage germination success of the barley seeds.

b Give evidence from the graph which suggests that other factors apart from exposure to gamma radiation also affect the percentage germination success.

c Predict the percentage of barley seeds that would germinate if 150 units of gamma radiation had been used.

Hint   For more on how to select information from a bar chart see page v.

9 The table shows the mass of a pea seedling at the start of germination and over the following 8 days.

Time after the start of germination (days)	Mass of seedling (g)
0	1·8
2	1·7
4	1·4
6	1·2
8	1·6

a The greatest **decrease** in mass was between:

A days 0 and 2

B days 2 and 4

C days 4 and 6

D days 6 and 8.

b On a piece of graph paper, draw a line graph to show these results.

10 A student investigated the effect of spacing on the germination of seeds.

The diagram shows the apparatus the student used.

The investigation could have been improved to make it valid by:

A putting the tubes in the dark

B repeating at different temperatures

C using damp cotton wool in both tubes

D using the same number of seeds in both tubes.

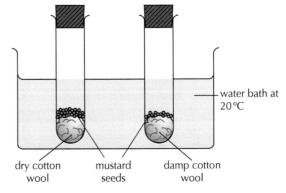

Hint   For more information on how to plan experiments see page vii.

11 The diagrams show six pots of seeds set up to investigate germination.

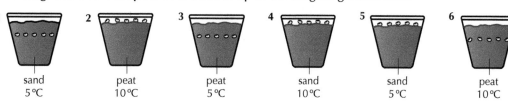

| 1 | 2 | 3 | 4 | 5 | 6 |
| sand 5°C | peat 10°C | peat 5°C | sand 10°C | sand 5°C | peat 10°C |

Which two pots selected by students should be compared to investigate the effect of temperature on germination?

A 1 and 2

B 2 and 3

C 4 and 5

D 5 and 6

12 The graph shows the effect of temperature on the germination of oat seeds and barley seeds.

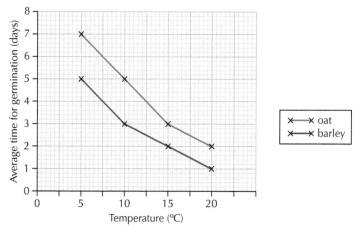

What is the average time for oat seeds to germinate at 5°C?

A 5 days

B 6 days

C 7 days

D 10 days

13 The shoot length of a germinating pea seedling was measured every 2 days.
The results are shown in the table.

Time (days)	Root length (mm)
0	0
2	6
4	11
6	17
8	24

a On a separate piece of graph paper, draw a line graph of this data.

b The shoot grew to a length of 24 mm over the 8 days. Calculate the average growth in shoot length per day.

14 An investigation into the conditions required for germination was carried out as shown.

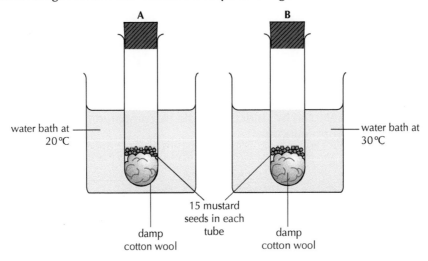

a State which variable was being investigated.

b 9 of the 15 seeds sown in tube **B** germinated.

 Calculate the percentage germination in this tube.

c Predict the effect on the number of seeds germinating in a third test tube if the water bath is set up at 60 °C.

15 The diagram shows an investigation into the effect of three minerals included in many fertilisers, nitrogen (N), phosphorus (P) and potassium (K), on the growth of a seedling.

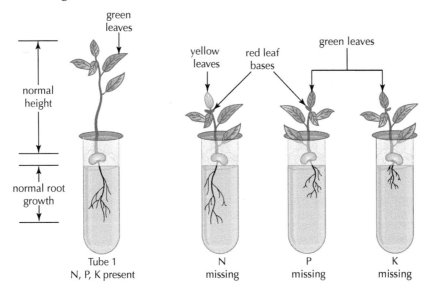

The solution in Tube 1 contained N, P and K.

The other tubes each contained a solution that had one mineral missing.

a Explain the purpose of Tube 1.

b State which minerals, when missing, result in red leaf bases.

c Describe the effects on the growth of the seedling if potassium (K) is missing from the solution.

16 The table and pie chart contain the same information about the diet of the British population.

Type of food	Percentage of diet
cereals	50
animal protein	25
fruit and vegetables	12·5
others	12·5

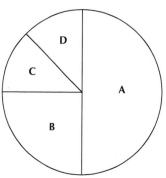

Which letter shown on the pie chart represents animal protein?

17 The table shows the recommended daily intake of food groups necessary for a healthy diet.

Food group	Recommended daily intake (measures)
carbohydrate	5–14
fruit/vegetables	5–9
dairy	2–3
meat	2–3
fat	0–3
sugar	1

1 measure = 25 grams (g)

a State which **two** food groups have a recommended intake of 50–75 g per day.

b Calculate the **maximum** number of recommended fat measures in **one week** which would be considered healthy.

c Calculate how many grams of sugar are recommended in **one week**.

18 The table shows the percentage composition of a veggie burger.

Component	Composition (%)
protein	50
fat	15
fibre	25
water	10

a Copy and complete the pie chart to show the information in the table.

b The veggie burger weighs 50 g.

Calculate the mass of protein present in the veggie burger.

c A beef burger contains 35% fat.

Calculate the simplest whole-number ratio of fat in a beef burger to fat in a veggie burger.

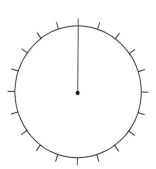

22 Maintaining stable body conditions

This exercise includes coverage of:

N4 Biological actions in response to internal and external changes to maintain stable body conditions

CL4 Body systems and cells SCN 4-12a

1 Give the meaning of the term **homeostasis**.

2 The core body temperature of a human is 37°C. If the core temperature starts to change, corrective responses are made by the skin.

   a Describe **one** corrective response to decreased core temperature.

   b Describe **one** corrective response to increased core temperature.

   c Name the condition caused by a drop in core body temperature to below 35°C.

3 The thermometer shows the body temperature of three patients.

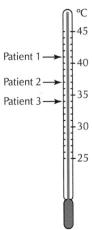

Which line in the table indicates the relationship between the body temperature of each patient and their health?

	Patient 1	Patient 2	Patient 3
A	healthy	fever	hypothermia
B	fever	healthy	hypothermia
C	fever	hypothermia	healthy
D	hypothermia	healthy	fever

4 **a** Name the condition caused by the failure of the body to control blood glucose concentration.

   b Copy and complete the following sentences by selecting the correct words from the choice brackets.

   The blood glucose level rises after a meal. In response, the hormone (**insulin / glucagon**) is released. This hormone causes the (**pancreas / liver**) to (**store / release**) glucose.

5 Which of the following pathways shows the correct response in blood vessels and in blood flow of the skin to an increase in body temperature?

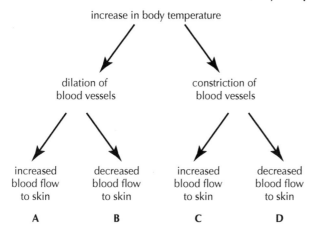

6 Skin is involved in temperature regulation.

The diagram represents a section of human skin.

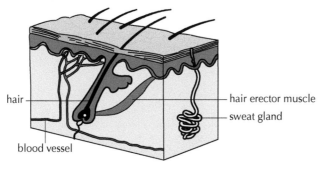

a A decrease in body temperature leads to a response by the skin blood vessels.

 i Describe the response of the skin blood vessels.

 ii Explain how this response helps to regulate body temperature.

b Referring to structures from the diagram, describe **two** other responses made by the skin to regulate body temperature.

c Copy and complete the following sentence by selecting the correct word from the choice brackets.

Human body temperature must be kept at 37 °C so that enzymes work at the (**fastest** / **slowest**) rate.

d Give the term used for the ability of the body to maintain a steady internal environment.

7 The body temperatures of two students were measured as they exercised for 2 hours. The results are shown in the table.

Name of student	Body temperature (°C)		
	At start	After 1 hour of exercise	After 2 hours of exercise
Euan	36·8	37·1	37·4
Sarah	37·0	37·1	37·5

a On a separate piece of graph paper, copy and complete the bar graph by:

   i providing a label for the vertical axis

   ii plotting the remaining results for both students.

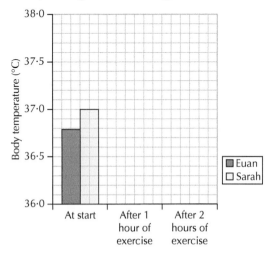

b Copy and complete the following sentences by selecting the correct words from the choice brackets.

The student whose body temperature increased more over 2 hours was (**Euan / Sarah**) and this student's body temperature increased by (**0·5 °C / 0·6 °C**).

8 An individual's blood glucose concentration was measured. The person then drank a glucose solution and their blood glucose concentration was measured at intervals over the next 150 minutes.

The graph shows the results.

a Calculate the increase in blood glucose concentration from 0 to 60 minutes.

b In which 30 minute period did the glucose concentration show the greatest decrease?

c Calculate the number of milligrams (mg) of glucose in 500 cm³ of blood at the start of the investigation.

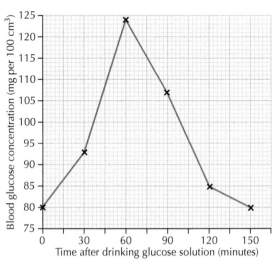

9 The bar chart shows the incidence of diabetes in people of different ages.

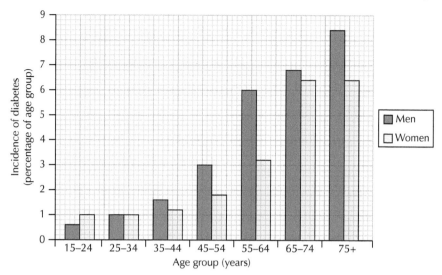

a Identify the age group with the highest incidence of diabetes.

b Give the percentage of diabetes in these groups:

   i men aged between 35 and 44

   ii women aged between 55 and 64.

c Identify the age group that shows no difference in the incidence of diabetes in men and women.

10 The graph shows the results of a glucose tolerance test in which two patients were given a standard glucose drink and their blood glucose levels were measured over the next 120 minutes.

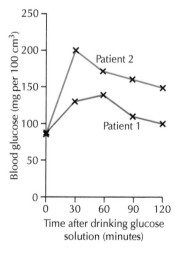

It was concluded that Patient 2 was diabetic.

Give **two** differences in the blood glucose concentration of these two patients after taking the glucose drink that provides evidence to support this conclusion.

23 Biodiversity, sampling and distribution of living organisms

N3 Sampling and identifying living things from different habitats to compare their biodiversity and suggest reasons for their distribution

CL3 Biodiversity and interdependence SCN 3-01a

1
  a Name the biological unit made up of a habitat and a community of living organisms.

  b Give the term used for the place where an organism lives.

  c Give **one** example of a habitat within a woodland ecosystem.

  d Name **two** abiotic factors that can affect the distribution of a species.

  e Give the meaning of the term **biodiversity**.

  f Give **two** examples of the importance of biodiversity to humans.

2 Give **one** example of a sampling technique and name **one** organism that it could be used to sample.

3 Copy and complete the following sentences, **choosing** the word from each choice bracket to give a correct statement.

    The (**habitat** / **community**) is the place where an organism lives.

    The (**population** / **biodiversity**) is the number and variety of different species in an ecosystem.

4 The grid contains some terms related to organisms and biodiversity.

A community	**B** ecosystem	**C** light intensity
D pitfall trap	**E** quadrat	**F** population

Use letters from the grid to match a term to each of the following statements:

  a All the organisms living in an ecosystem

  b A piece of equipment that could be used to sample a species of plant or slow-moving animals in a field

  c An abiotic factor that could affect the distribution of organisms living in an area

5 A comparison was made between the types of invertebrate animals living on the branches and leaves of an oak tree with those living on a beech tree.

Samples were collected as shown.

  a Give **two** variables that should be kept constant to make the comparison valid when using this technique on the two different trees.

  b The samples collected were not representative of all the invertebrates living on the trees.

    Suggest a reason for this.

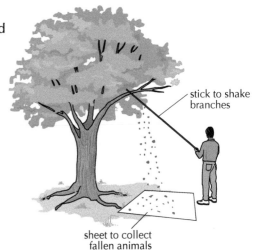

stick to shake branches

sheet to collect fallen animals

6 During a woodland survey, a group of students measured some abiotic factors.

Measurements they took included the temperature of the soil and the air.

a Name **one** abiotic factor, other than temperature, which they could have measured in the woodland and describe the method of measuring this factor.

b During the survey, the students sampled the leaf litter in the woodland using pitfall traps. When they checked the traps 4 days after setting them up, the students found they were all empty.

Describe **one** error the students might have made which would explain why there were no invertebrates in the traps.

c The leaf litter in the woodland was sampled and the table shows the number and types of invertebrates found.

Invertebrates	Number found
woodlice	40
beetles	25
spiders	25
snails	10

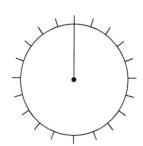

Use the information from the table to copy and complete a pie chart as shown.

d The students saw a large number of wasps in the woodland.

Give **one** reason why no wasps were collected with the invertebrates.

7 **a** A group of students set pitfall traps in the school gardens to sample invertebrates living there.

All the traps were left for the same length of time.

The results are shown in the table.

Pitfall trap number	Number of each type of invertebrate trapped			
	Spider	Beetle	Snail	Woodlouse
1	10	6	3	0
2	5	2	2	3
3	6	1	4	4

i Calculate the average number of spiders found in the traps.

Hint   For more information on how to calculate an average see page vi.

ii Calculate the difference in the total number of spiders collected compared to the number of woodlice.

iii Suggest what could be done to increase the reliability of the results.

Hint   For more information on how to improve reliability in an experiment see page vii.

b Give **one** precaution that must be taken when setting up a pitfall trap.

8 The biological key shown describes some of the characteristics of insects that are beneficial to gardeners.

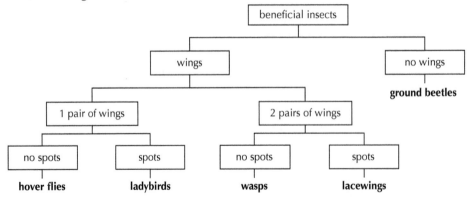

a Copy and complete the table using the information from the key.

Beneficial insect	Number of pairs of wings	Spots
	1	no
ground beetles		no
ladybirds	1	
	2	no
lacewings		

b Using information from the key, state the difference between ladybirds and lacewings.

9 A Tullgren funnel is used to sample the number of animals living in leaf litter as shown. The animals in the litter move away from the light and fall into the collecting pot.

A student used a Tullgren funnel to sample the number of millipedes living in leaf litter in two areas of a woodland. The student took leaf litter from five quadrats in the centre of the wood and from five quadrats near the edge of the wood.

The table shows the student's results.

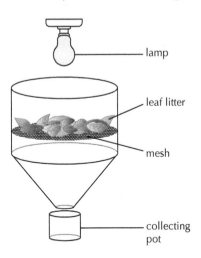

Quadrat	Number of millipedes per m² of leaf litter	
	Centre of woodland	Edge of woodland
1	10	4
2	8	2
3	8	3
4	13	6
5	12	4

a One factor that the millipedes respond to in the Tullgren funnel is light.

Suggest **one** other abiotic factor that might cause millipedes to fall into the collecting pot.

b State the total difference in the number of millipedes found in the leaf litter samples from the two areas of the woodland and suggest a reason for this difference.

10 Three students were asked to estimate the population size of a plant species in an area using a quadrat.

The diagram shows where each student placed their quadrat in the area.

Student A   Student B   Student C

a State which student would obtain the most reliable estimate.

  Give a reason for your answer.

b Name **one** factor that could affect the population size of the plant species.

11 The animals present in a sample of leaf litter were counted.

Animals	Number in sample
ground beetles	10
woodlice	35
slugs	5
centipedes	10
others	10

What percentage of animals in the sample are woodlice?

A 35%   **B** 50%

C 65%   **D** 70%

> **Hint** For more information on how to calculate a percentage see page vi.

12 A survey was carried out on the number of mussels attached to rocks on a seashore.

The positions of the mussels are shown by squares in the diagram.

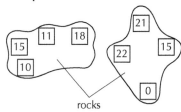

rocks

The numbers of mussels at each position are shown in the squares.

What is the average number of mussels found per square?

A 14   **B** 16

C 56   **D** 112

This exercise includes coverage of:

N4 Animal and plant species depend on each other

CL4 Biodiversity and interdependence SCN 4-01a

 Give **two** examples of how animal and plant species depend on each other.

 The diagram shows part of a food web in a freshwater loch.

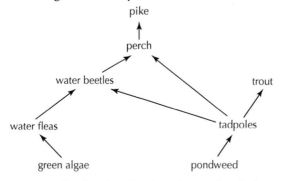

    a From the food web, identify **one** food chain with **five** species.

    b Explain what the arrows in a food chain represent.

    c Identify the species that are producers.

    d Name **two** species from the food web that are in competition with each other.

    e Describe the effect on other species in the web if the tadpoles were to die out.

 The diagram shows a food web from a moorland ecosystem.

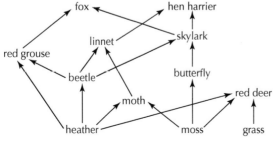

    a Use the words **increase**, **decrease** or **stay the same** to predict the effect on the numbers of butterflies **and** red grouse if the skylarks were removed from the food web.

    Give the reasons for your answers.

    b Copy and complete the table, inserting the missing biotic factors.

Biotic factor	Example from the moorland ecosystem
	Hen harriers chase and catch skylarks and linnets.
	Every few years, red grouse populations are infected with worms which live in their gut.
	Red grouse and red deer eat some of the same moorland plants.

    c Give the term that describes the role an organism has within its community in an ecosystem.

4 The diagram shows part of an Antarctic food web.

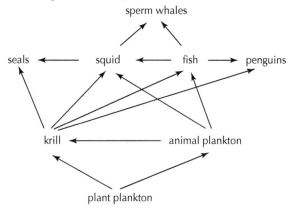

a Explain why a decrease in sperm whale numbers may lead to an increase in the seal population.

b Give the meaning of the phrase **population of squid**.

c Describe how penguins depend on plant plankton.

d Name **one** biotic factor that would exist between squid and fish.

5 Limpets are small animals that feed on the green algae that grow on rocks on seashores.

Oystercatchers are birds that feed on limpets.

In a study in part of the USA, where three limpet species are common, the limpets were protected from oystercatchers by large wire cages. After 2 years the number of limpets in this area was compared with the number of limpets in an area without cages, where oystercatchers were present.

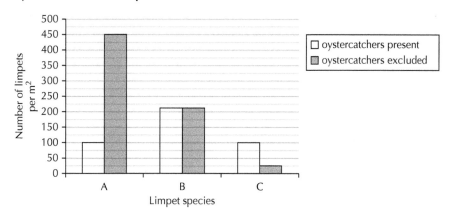

a Give the number of species A present when oystercatchers were excluded.

b Identify evidence that suggests oystercatchers don't eat species B.

c Calculate the difference in the number of species C eaten with and without the wire cages.

6 Use the four food chains given here to construct a food web.

fir tree seeds → red squirrel → great horned owl

fir tree seeds → red squirrel → pine marten

fir tree seeds → deer mouse → pine marten

fir tree seeds → deer mouse → skunk → great horned owl

25 Impacts on biodiversity

N4 Impact of population growth and natural hazards on biodiversity

CL4 Biodiversity and interdependence SCN 4-01a

 The human population is increasing at an ever-faster rate.

The graph shows the increase in human population between years 1000 and 2000 of the Common Era (CE).

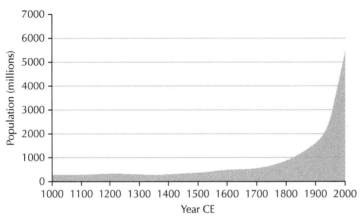

a Describe how the human population has grown over the last thousand years.

b Give **two** reasons why the human population has been able to grow so quickly.

c Name **two** resources needed by a growing population.

2 **a** State the effect that increasing human population has had on biodiversity on Earth.

b Give **two** threats to biodiversity that are caused by human activities.

c Give **two** natural hazards that can threaten biodiversity.

d Describe **one** way in which humans are trying to conserve biodiversity.

3 State the meaning of the following terms:

a ecological footprint

b genetic pollution.

4 Intensive agriculture methods can result in habitat destruction and involve the use of chemicals.

Describe each of these issues and say how it has had an impact on biodiversity:

a habitat destruction

b use of chemicals in agriculture.

5 Identify **one** example of how human activity changes a biotic factor and could affect biodiversity.

6 Identify **one** example of how a human activity changes an abiotic factor and could affect biodiversity.

7 The deforestation of tropical rainforests continues to cause great concern in some parts of the world because of its impact on biodiversity.

In the 5 years between 2000 and 2005, Africa lost 3300 hectares per year. Asia lost 2800 hectares per year and South America lost 4000 hectares per year.

a Present this information in a table.

b Calculate the total number of hectares of rainforest that were lost between 2000 and 2005 inclusive. (Remember: each of the figures given is **per year**.)

8 Read the passage and use the information given to answer the questions.

Coral reefs are an important habitat. Thousands of marine plants and animals survive only in reefs. Reefs also protect some coastlines from erosion by the sea.

Coral reefs are easily damaged and take many years to recover. Most of the world's coral reefs have now been damaged. In some regions, such as the Philippines, they have been completely destroyed. The main threats to the reefs come from tourism and pollution. More problems are caused by uncontrolled forest clearing. If trees are cut down, rivers can wash the soil down to the sea. The corals can be buried by mud and sand, and this kills the reef.

a Give **two** reasons why coral reefs are important.

b Explain why deforestation can damage coral reefs.

c Other than deforestation, give **one** other threat to the reefs.

9 A study carried out to investigate deforestation of tropical rainforests revealed that 14 000 square kilometres were chopped down in Brazil. In the same year, 6000 square kilometres were cut down in Columbia. Mexico lost 7000 square kilometres. In Peru, the area of rainforest cut down was 3000 square kilometres.

Use this information to draw a bar chart showing the area of rainforest lost (square kilometres) for each country.

> Hint   For more information on how to present information see page vi.

26 Nitrogen cycle

This exercise includes coverage of:

N4 Nitrogen cycle

CL4 Biodiversity and interdependence SCN 4-03a

1. The diagrams represent part of the nitrogen cycle.

   Which diagram shows the correct sequence of events in this part of the nitrogen cycle?

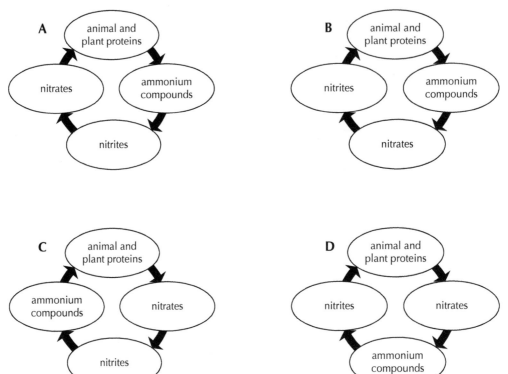

2. Copy and complete, **selecting** the correct words from each set of choice brackets to make the following sentences correct.

   a The addition of nitrogen to the soil from the atmosphere is called (**nitrogen fixation / nitrification**).

   b The conversion of ammonium to nitrate in the soil is called (**nitrification / denitrification**).

   c Plants absorb nitrate from the soil and use it in the synthesis of (**carbohydrate / protein**).

   d In waterlogged conditions, (**denitrifying / nitrifying**) bacteria remove nitrogen from soil.

3. Name **two** types of microorganism that are vital for the nitrogen cycle.

4 The diagram shows some of the stages in the nitrogen cycle.

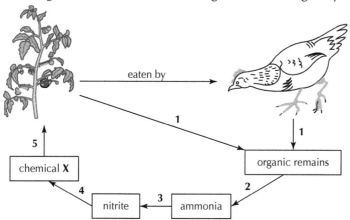

a Copy and complete the table by giving a number from the diagram to match each of the named stages.

Stage	Number
absorption	
death	
nitrification	
decomposition	

b Name chemical **X**.

c Name the type of organism responsible for stage **3**.

5 The following list gives some of the stages involved in the nitrogen cycle.

   1 Production of plant protein

   2 Absorption of nitrogen compounds into plants

   3 Nitrates produced in the soil

   4 Ammonium compounds produced from soil organic matter

   5 Nitrites produced in the soil

   6 Death of plants

a Copy and complete the flow chart using the numbers from the list to show the correct sequence of stages.

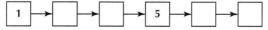

b Three of the stages involve the action of bacteria.

Give the numbers of any **two** of these stages.

6 The recycling of nitrogen in ecosystems depends on the action of bacteria.

Describe the role of each of the following bacteria in the nitrogen cycle.

a Nitrifying bacteria

b Denitrifying bacteria

c Root nodule bacteria

7 Nitrogen is an important element in living organisms.

The diagram shows stages in the nitrogen cycle in an ecosystem.

a The numbers in the diagram represent stages in the transfer of nitrogen in an ecosystem.

  i Give the number that indicates the stage at which death and decay occurs.

  ii Give the number that indicates the denitrification stage.

b Nitrogen-fixing bacteria are involved in stage **1**.

State **one** place where these microorganisms can be found.

c Identify chemical **R** and explain its importance to plants.

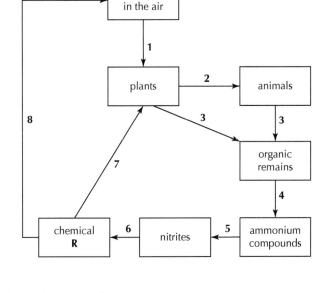

8 The graph shows the change in plant growth when different masses of nitrate fertiliser are added to fields.

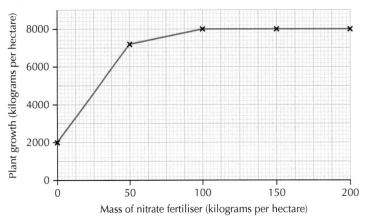

a Give the mass of nitrate fertiliser at which it stops being a limiting factor in the growth of the plant.

b Predict the plant growth when 25 kg of nitrate fertiliser was applied.

> **Hint** For more information on how to make a prediction using a line graph see page viii.

c Calculate how many times the plant growth increased when the mass of nitrate fertiliser was increased from 0 to 100 kg per hectare.

> **Hint** For more on how to select information from a line graph see page v.

1 The list shows different types of adaptation found in animals.

> **A** structural
>
> **B** physiological
>
> **C** behavioural

Use letters from the list to match the type of adaptation with the following examples.

a Salmon have glands in their gills which excrete salt when they are in sea water.

b Polar bears have a thick fatty layer that insulates the body.

c The kangaroo rat is nocturnal to avoid the heat of the day.

d Polar bears have an acute sense of smell to detect seals.

2 Explain the following adaptations that are found in some cactus plants.

a They have spines instead of leaves.

b Their pores open at night instead of during the day.

3 Cactus plants are adapted to survive in hot, dry conditions. They have shallow, widespread root systems, the ability to store water in their stems, spines for shade, a waxy coating and no leaves.

a Explain how having no leaves can help a cactus survive in hot, dry conditions.

b Suggest how a shallow, widespread root system would help a cactus to survive in a desert environment.

c Other than reducing its surface area, suggest **one** advantage to cactus plants of having spines.

4 Jerboas are desert mammals that sleep in underground burrows during the hot day and come out during the cold night.

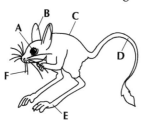

a Name the type of adaptation that causes jerboas to be active at night.

b For each statement, give the letter from the diagram of an adaptation that matches.

> **i** Helps to insulate the jerboa
>
> **ii** Helps the jerboa to detect insects in the dark
>
> **iii** Helps the jerboa to hop quickly to escape predators
>
> **iv** Helps the jerboa to keep its balance when hopping
>
> **v** Helps the jerboa to know the width of its underground burrow in the dark

5 Emperor penguins live in the southern polar regions. The temperature there can be as low as –30 °C.

Their adaptations enable them to survive in this cold climate.

a Penguins have soft downy feathers and a thick layer of fat just below the skin.

Suggest how these features help penguins to survive.

b Penguins huddle together in tightly packed groups.

Explain how this behaviour is an advantage to penguins.

6 Woodpigeons often feed in small groups.

The woodpigeons use their eyes to spot an approaching sparrowhawk and fly up to escape when one is seen.

The table gives information about the success that a sparrowhawk has in catching woodpigeons in different group sizes.

Number of woodpigeons in group	Average distance at which woodpigeons first see sparrowhawk (metres)	Success rate of a sparrowhawk catching a woodpigeon (%)
1	3	80
2–10	16	58
11–50	30	18
> 50	40	6

a Present selected information in the table as a bar chart to show how the success rate of a hawk catching a pigeon changes with the number of pigeons.

b Use the information in the table to:

i describe the relationship between the size of a group of woodpigeons and the success rate of the sparrowhawk

ii suggest how larger groups are able to reduce the success rate of sparrowhawks.

7 Many animals live on rocky shores. Some live high on the shore, some live much lower down the shore.

The diagram illustrates where you might find some of these animals.

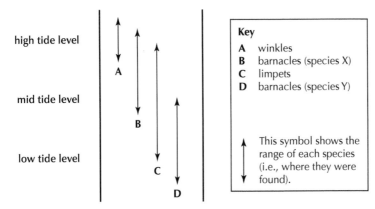

high tide level

mid tide level

low tide level

A

B

C

D

Key

A winkles
B barnacles (species X)
C limpets
D barnacles (species Y)

This symbol shows the range of each species (i.e., where they were found).

a Suggest which of the four species is better adapted to survive being out of the water for long periods of time.

b State which species can survive the greatest range of conditions.

8 Many species of insects live in rivers.

A student carried out an investigation to find out how the rate of water flow at six sites in a river affected the numbers of two species of insect, **A** and **B**.

The table shows the results.

Site	Water flow rate (cm/s)	Number of insects	
		Species A	Species B
1	10	6	0
2	20	5	1
3	40	4	2
4	60	2	4
5	80	1	6
6	90	0	11

a Calculate the average number of species **A** from all six sites.

b Identify the increase in water flow rate that caused the greatest change in the number of species **B**.

c Give **one** conclusion that can be drawn from the results.

28 Chemicals and food production

This exercise includes coverage of:

N3 Different types of chemicals in agriculture, the alternatives and their impact on global food production

CL3 Biodiversity and interdependence SCN 3-03a

1. Name the agricultural chemicals that are added to the soil to increase nutrient levels and crop yield.

2. Explain why pests reduce crop yields.

3. Explain why farmers use artificial chemicals to increase their crop yields.

4. Name the type of farming that avoids the use of artificial agricultural chemicals.

5. Give **one** example of a natural fertiliser.

6. Give the term used for the introduction of a natural predator to control pests.

7. Explain why introducing natural predators may work better **and** be safer in greenhouses or polytunnels than in open fields.

8. Some rice farmers use ducks as a method of biological control.

   The ducks help rice plants to grow because they eat insects and weeds in the paddy fields.

   a i Suggest how, by eating insects, the ducks help rice plants to grow bigger.

   ii Explain how the ducks, by eating weeds, help rice plants to grow bigger.

   b The ducks produce droppings which fall into the water in the paddy fields.

   Explain why droppings from the ducks help rice plants to grow bigger.

9. A gardener examined his plants and rated their health.

   The table shows information about the health of the plants.

Health	Percentage of plants
healthy	25
insect infection	20
fungal infection	15
both insect and fungal infections	40

   a Copy and complete the pie chart using the information in the table.

   b There were 200 plants in the garden.

   Calculate the number of plants that had any type of infection.

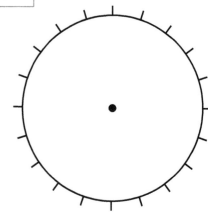

10 Some insects help gardeners by eating pests which attack their plants.

The table shows some of these beneficial insects and the pests that they eat.

a Identify all of the beneficial insects that could be used to treat plants which are attacked by aphids.

b Identify all of the beneficial insects which could be used to treat plants that are attacked by caterpillars.

Beneficial insect	Pests eaten
hoverflies	leafhoppers, caterpillars
ground beetles	snails, slugs
ladybirds	aphids
wasps	caterpillars, grubs
lacewings	aphids

c Some gardeners use insecticides to control pests.

Predict the effect the use of the chemicals would have on beneficial insects.

11 Some varieties of potato plant are eaten by beetles, reducing their yield.

A genetically modified (GM) beetle-resistant variety of potato plant was developed.

The yields of both varieties were compared by growing them in two separate fields.

The results are shown in the graph.

a Identify **one** variable that would have to be kept the same between the two fields used to grow the two varieties to allow a fair comparison to be made.

b Give **one** conclusion from the results of this investigation.

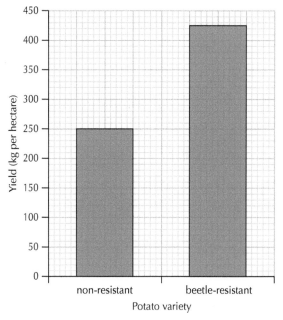

12 The bar graph shows the changes in wheat yield over a 50-year period.

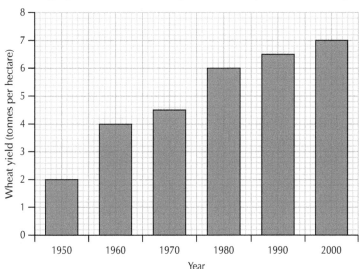

a Give the 10-year period that showed the greatest increase in wheat yield.

b Calculate the increase in yield between 1960 and 1980.

c Calculate the increase in yield over the whole period.

13 The sparrowhawk is a bird of prey that feeds on woodpigeons and blue tits.
Blue tits eat insects.

An area was sprayed with insecticide.
The concentration of insecticide found
in the flesh of each bird in parts
per million (ppm) was investigated
one year after the spraying and the results are
shown in the table.

Bird	Insecticide concentration (ppm)
sparrowhawk	3·2
woodpigeon	1·6
blue tit	0·4

a Present the information in the table as a bar chart.

b The woodpigeon eats only plants.

   Suggest why it has insecticide in its body.

c Calculate how many times greater the insecticide concentration is in the sparrowhawk compared to the insecticide concentration in the blue tit.

d The sparrowhawk feeds on woodpigeons and blue tits.

   i Explain why the sparrowhawk has a higher concentration of insecticide in its body than either the woodpigeon or the blue tit.

   ii Explain why sparrowhawks may be damaged by the concentration of insecticide in their bodies but woodpigeons and blue tits might not.

14 Red spider mites are pests on crops, such as tomatoes, growing in greenhouses in the UK. They feed on the leaves and destroy the plants. Predatory mites feed on red spider mites.

Scientists investigated the use of predatory mites to control red spider mites on tomato plants in a greenhouse.

The bar chart shows their results.

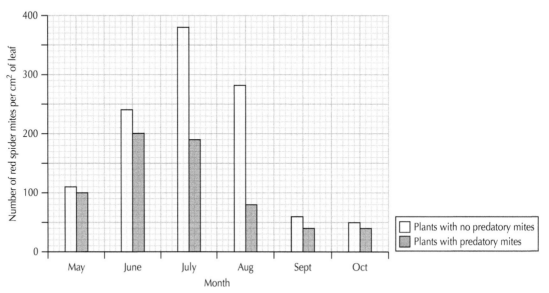

a The scientists concluded that using predatory mites is an effective way to control red spider mites.

   Give evidence that supports this conclusion.

b Calculate the decrease in red spider mite numbers due to predatory mites in the month of August.

29 Fertilisers

N4 Fertiliser design and the environmental impact of their use

CL4 Biodiversity and interdependence SCN 4-02a, SCN 4-03a

1 Use the words provided in the list to copy and complete the following sentences.

peat   artificial   nitrate   compost   fertiliser   manure

a When crops grow and are harvested, _ _ _ _ _ _ _ is removed from the soil. In agriculture this is replaced by adding _ _ _ _ _ _ _ _ _ _ to improve crop yield.

b Natural fertilisers include _ _ _ _ _ _ , _ _ _ _ _ _ _ and _ _ _ _ .

c _ _ _ _ _ _ _ _ _ _ fertilisers are made in factories from inorganic substances.

2 When crops are harvested nitrogen is removed from the nitrogen cycle.

a Give **one** example of a natural method that is used to replace the lost nitrogen.

b State what is meant by an **artificial fertiliser**.

3 The list shows steps in a process caused when fertilisers from a field wash into a pond.

     A Loss of oxygen from water

     B Decomposition of dead plants

     C Death of animals

     C Blocking of light

     E Death of larger pond plants

     F Rapid growth of algae

Copy and complete the flow chart to show the order in which these events would occur using letters from the list.

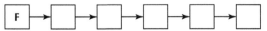

4 **a** The table shows the mineral composition of an artificial fertiliser.

Mineral (units)		
Nitrogen (N)	Phosphorus (P)	Potassium (K)
10	5	5

Copy and complete the pie chart using the information in the table.

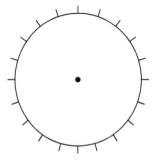

b Another fertiliser contains 140 g nitrogen, 210 g phosphorus and 140 g potassium.

Copy and complete the pie chart using the information in the table.

Calculate the simplest whole number ratio of nitrogen, phosphorus and potassium in this fertiliser.

Hint   For more information on how to calculate a ratio see page vi.

5 A student set up an experiment to investigate the effect of minerals on the root growth of duckweed seedlings.

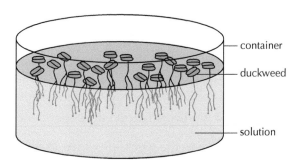

a 20 duckweed seedlings were used in the beaker.

Explain why this was good experimental procedure.

> **Hint** For more information on how to improve reliability in an experiment see page vii.

b The root length of each seedling was measured every 5 days and the average length of the roots was calculated.

The results are shown in the table.

On a separate piece of graph paper, draw a line graph of the average length of roots (mm) against time (days).

Time (days)	Average length of roots (mm)
0	0
5	8
10	16
15	22
20	27

c The student set up a second beaker exactly the same as the beaker shown, except that the water did not contain any minerals.

Explain why the student set up this second beaker.

> **Hint** For more information on experimental controls see page vii.

6 A student investigated the growth of tomato plants over a two-month period.

a In one investigation, three tomato plants were grown without fertiliser.

The increase in the height of each plant, after 2 months, is shown in the table.

Plant	Increase in height of tomato plants (cm)
1	9·8
2	10·5
3	10·0

Calculate the average increase in the height of these plants.

b In a second investigation, another three tomato plants of the same variety and stage of growth were each given a different fertiliser, A, B or C.

The average increase in the height of each plant, after 2 months, is shown in the table.

Fertiliser	Average increase in height of tomato plants (cm)
A	20·4
B	14·6
C	10·6

Describe the effect of these fertilisers on the height of the tomato plants.

7 Farmers add fertiliser to their crops to increase the yield. Fertilisers usually contain nitrate, phosphate and potassium.

The table shows crop yield when fertilisers lacking one of these three minerals were applied to crops.

Crop	Yield (%)			
	No nitrate	No phosphate	No potassium	All three minerals added
rice	63	97	99	100
barley	52	68	72	100
wheat	46	69	72	100
potato	47	47	70	100

a Identify the mineral that has the greatest effect on wheat yield.

b State which crop is most affected by the lack of phosphate.

8 An investigation was carried out to determine the effects of nitrate concentration on plant growth using duckweed. This plant reproduces asexually by repeatedly dividing into two.

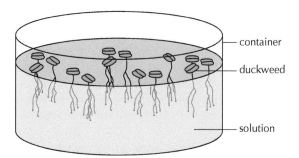

Ten plants were added to beakers containing different concentrations of nitrate. The numbers of duckweed plants were counted after one week.

The results are shown in the table.

Beaker	Concentration of nitrate (M)	Number of plants after one week
1	0·2	12
2	0·4	14
3	0·6	16

a Give **one** conclusion that can be made from the results of this investigation.

b Give **two** factors that should have been kept constant at each concentration of nitrate.

c Describe a suitable control for this investigation.

9 A farmer wanted to grow wheat in three of his fields. Before planting, he took soil samples and analysed them for the content of the three mineral nutrients, nitrate, potassium and phosphate.

The results are shown in the bar chart.

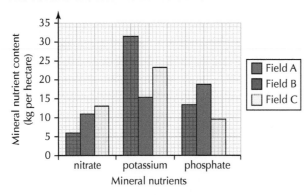

The table gives the minimum value of each mineral needed for the healthy growth of the wheat plants.

Mineral nutrient	Minimum value needed for healthy growth of wheat (kg per hectare)
nitrate	6·0
potassium	17·0
phosphate	12·0

Use the information in the bar chart and table to answer the following questions.

> **Hint** For more on how to select information from a bar chart see page v.

a State which field could be used by the farmer to grow a healthy wheat crop without the addition of any fertiliser.

b Identify **one** field that would not be suitable to grow wheat without additional fertiliser and give a reason for your answer.

c Calculate the average nitrate content present in the soil of the three fields.

30 Learned behaviour

N4 Learned behaviour and survival

CL4 Biodiversity and interdependence SCN 4-12b

1. Describe what is meant by **innate behaviour**.

2. Give **one** example of innate behaviour.

3. Describe what is meant by **learned behaviour**.

4. Give **one** example of a category of learned behaviour.

5. Describe what is meant by **habituation**.

6. Give **one** example of habituation.

7. Which of the following experiments could be used to show the response of an earthworm to temperature?

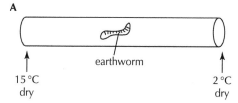

A

earthworm

15 °C
dry

2 °C
dry

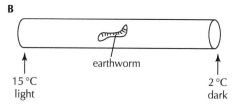

B

earthworm

15 °C
light

2 °C
dark

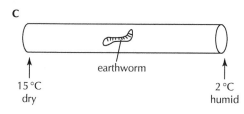

C

earthworm

15 °C
dry

2 °C
humid

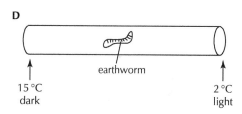

D

earthworm

15 °C
dark

2 °C
light

8. The table gives the approximate distances of the annual migrations of various animals.

Animal	Approximate distance of annual migration (miles)
Arctic tern	21 000
gray whale	12 000
snow goose	5 000
monarch butterfly	2 000
caribou	1 000

   a On a separate piece of graph paper, use the information in the table to draw a bar chart.

   > **Hint** For more information on how to present information, see page vi.

   b Each year the monarch butterfly migrates from North America to Mexico and back.

   It flies at an average speed of 10 miles per hour.

   Calculate how long it takes to fly the North-America-to-Mexico stage of its migration.

9 An investigation was carried out into the response of flour beetles to humidity.

Two T-shaped glass tubes were set up as shown.

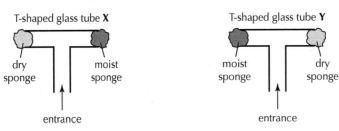

Each T-shaped tube was left for 10 minutes before one beetle was placed at the entrance.

The direction in which the beetle turned was recorded.

This was repeated for a total of 25 beetles using a different beetle and a new T-shaped tube each time.

The results for the investigation are shown in the table.

	Tube			
	X		Y	
Direction turned	left	right	left	right
Humidity	dry	moist	moist	dry
Number of beetles	21	4	5	20

a Which of the following is the best conclusion to draw from this investigation?

    A Most flour beetles turn left.

    B Most flour beetles turn right.

    C Most flour beetles turn to dry areas.

    D Most flour beetles turn to moist areas.

> **Hint** For more information on how to evaluate an experiment see page viii.

b The diagram shows that tubes **X** and **Y** were set up differently.

    Describe how this improves the validity of the investigation.

c Explain the purpose of leaving each tube for 10 minutes before placing a beetle at the entrance.

d Suggest a reason why a new T-tube was used for each beetle, rather than using the same tube repeatedly.

e Calculate the total percentage of beetles that turned towards the moist ends in the investigation.

> **Hint** For more information on how to calculate a percentage see page vi.

10 An experiment was set up to study the response of woodlice to light.

Ten woodlice were placed in a glass tube. After 5 minutes one end of the tube was covered with black paper to make it dark. The number of woodlice in light and dark was then recorded every minute for 5 minutes.

The diagram shows the apparatus used.

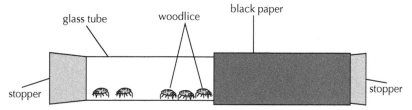

The table shows the results of the experiment.

Time (minutes)	Number of woodlice	
	In light	In dark
0	5	5
1	6	4
2	4	6
3	3	7
4	2	8
5	1	9

a Name **one** environmental condition that should be kept constant in this investigation.

b Explain why the woodlice were left for 5 minutes before the black paper was placed on the tube.

c Give **one** conclusion that can be drawn from the results of this experiment.

d A student repeated this experiment.

Describe how the design could be changed to make the results more reliable.

11 Flatworms are animals that live in freshwater streams.

20 flatworms were placed in the centre of a tray containing water. The tray had black and white squares painted on the bottom.

The diagram shows the position of the flatworms 1 hour later.

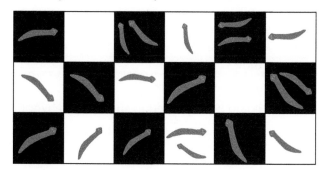

= flatworm

a Calculate the percentage of flatworms that were found on black squares.

b Suggest why this behaviour may help flatworms survive in the streams where they live.

12 An investigation to demonstrate the responses of woodlice to light was carried out in a choice chamber. Half of the choice chamber was covered in black paper and the other half left in light.

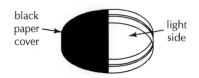

Ten woodlice were introduced into the choice chamber. The number of woodlice in each side was counted every 2 minutes for 10 minutes.

The graph shows the results of this investigation.

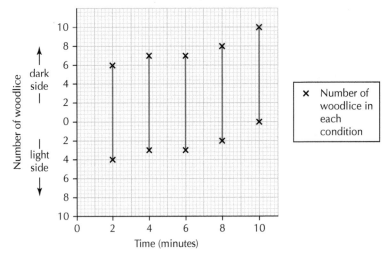

a Give **two** environmental conditions that should be kept constant in this investigation.

b State the number of woodlice in the light at 6 minutes.

c Give **one** conclusion that can be drawn from the results of this investigation.

13 An investigation was set up as shown to study the behaviour of slugs.

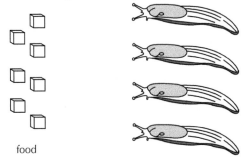

food

During the investigation the slugs moved towards the food.

a Two possible hypotheses for the movement of the slugs are:

1 The slugs saw the food and moved towards it.

2 The slugs smelled the food and moved towards it.

Suggest how the investigation could be improved to show which hypothesis was correct.

b Explain why it was good experimental practice to use four slugs rather than just one.